C000173515

Emotional In

The Empath Experience, Anger Management and
the Art of Happiness

(Your Social Intelligence by Learning to Use
Several Techniques on Improving Your Interaction
With Others)

Linda Caruso

Published by Kevin Dennis

Linda Caruso

All Rights Reserved

Emotional Intelligence: The Empath Experience, Anger Management and the Art of Happiness (Your Social Intelligence by Learning to Use Several Techniques on Improving Your Interaction With Others)

ISBN 978-1-989965-31-3

Legal & Disclaimer

The information contained in this book is not designed to replace or take the place of any form of medicine or professional medical advice. The information in this book has been provided for educational and entertainment purposes only.

The information contained in this book has been compiled from sources deemed reliable, and it is accurate to the best of the Author's knowledge; however, the Author cannot guarantee its accuracy and validity and cannot be held liable for any errors or omissions. Changes are periodically made to this book. You must consult your doctor or get professional medical advice before using any of the suggested remedies, techniques, or information in this book.

Upon using the information contained in this book, you agree to hold harmless the Author from and against any damages, costs, and expenses, including any legal fees potentially resulting from the application of any of the information provided by this guide. This disclaimer applies to any damages or injury caused by the use and application, whether directly or indirectly, of any advice or information presented, whether for breach of contract, tort, negligence, personal injury, criminal intent, or under any other cause of action.

You agree to accept all risks of using the information presented inside this book. You need to consult a professional medical practitioner in order to ensure you are both able and healthy enough to participate in this program.

TABLE OF CONTENTS

Introduction

Have you ever thought about why, when buying a new phone, laptop or TV, a person more often prefers a well-known brand product that is more expensive than a much cheaper analogue of an unpopular brand? At the same time, technical specifications, appearance, warranty are almost the same, so it is far from always possible to justify this with favorable conditions or better quality. But did it happen that, having received a salary, you went shopping, spontaneously bought yourself something, and, after a while, thought about the expediency of this purchase and blamed yourself? It wasn't worth it, because there are a lot of such people.

Those who in actions are guided by emotions and impulses, and not by logic. This may sound a little offensive, but they have not developed enough emotional intelligence the ability to use and use their emotions, to manage them. But there is good news, you can train him!

Emotional intelligence and the collapse of the classical economy

The starting point for a detailed study of the problems of emotional intelligence was 2002. Of course, the field of human emotions interested scientists constantly, but in the past few yearsthe Nobel Prize in Economics was awarded to psychologists D. Kahneman and W. Smith for research in behavioral economics. If we talk about its results briefly, it was proved that most often people, when making decisions, are guided not by logical intelligence, but by emotions.

In support of this fact, a curious experiment was cited: the acquisition and loss of the same amount of money causes a person to experience different strengths. So, when acquiring, for example, $ 100, the degree of satisfaction is emotionally less than the loss of the same amount.

This is described in much more detail in the monograph by E. Khlevna and L. Yuzhaninova, "Where is your magic button?" How to develop emotional intelligence. " In it, the authors show the conviction that, as described above, the recognition of the merits of psychologists "was triggered by the trident on the classical economy." Behavioral, on the other hand, was largely based on an understanding of the essence of emotional intelligence, which J. Mayer and P. Salovei, professors of Yale University, have been studying since 1990.

Under the term "emotional intelligence" (EQ, as opposed to IQ) in their writings describes the person's ability to recognize emotions, to achieve and generate them in such a way as to promote thinking, understanding of emotions and what they mean, and, accordingly, to manage them in such a way as to promote their emotional and intellectual growth.

Why does this person need this ability?

Firstly, for effective communication with people. Not a single manager, HR manager, businessman, PR manager or advertiser can do without it. The dependence of the decisions made on the emotional background is true in all cases, which is why now so many cute cats and dogs convince us from TV screens about the need to make some kind of purchase. The example is a little exaggerated, but the general idea conveys well. "Virus", "word of mouth",

Secondly, the developed emotional intelligence makes it possible not to fall into commercial networks, resist manipulation, and set priorities and goals correctly.

More recently, there are published material about empathy, and you may have noticed some similarities between it and emotional intelligence. Indeed, empathy, as the ability to understand and empathize with the emotions of others, is one of the components of EQ. Along with self-government, social skills and self-awareness.

How to develop emotional intelligence

A high level of EQ allows a person to develop more productively in both personal and professional plans, manage stress and build effective communication with others. Work on its development will at least teach you to understand the background of some of your unconscious actions.

Notice your emotional reactions. Pay attention to what is happening to and around you, and try to understand how you feel about these phenomena on an emotional level. Do not ignore your feelings, as you lose an important part of the incoming information.

Listen to your body language. Do not suppress physical manifestations of feelings. Our mind and body are closely connected and, having learned to understand this connection, you can easily "read" identical feelings and experiences of others.

Watch how your emotions and behavior are related. Anger makes us raise our voices, embarrassment makes us slurredly. These are just the most obvious examples, but when you understand the connection between feelings and behavior, you will learn how to deal with them and use them to your advantage.

Do not suppress your feelings. Not in the sense that every time someone steps on your foot in public transport, you should start screaming. But negative emotions are as much part of an adequate reaction to what is happening as positive ones. Analyze your feelings, look for a way out and never hide insults and sorrows inside yourself.

Develop emotional memory. Keep a special diary and write down your emotional reactions there. Rereading it over time, you will be able to look at yourself from the side, to understand whether they have acted correctly or not, to correct your future behavior.

Practice your desired reactions. You cannot force yourself to experience or not to experience any emotions, but you can decide how to react to them. Are you missing out on a trifle? Make a conclusion, and next time keep yourself in control, even if it's difficult.

Be open and friendly in relationships. These two qualities practically go hand in hand with emotional intelligence.

Develop empathy skills. This will teach you to understand the feelings of other people and share your emotions with them.

Learn to listen. Both literally and figuratively. Not only words have meaning, but also tone, expression, body language at the time of speech. With a certain degree of mastery in these parameters, you can even learn to distinguish between truth and falsehood.

Be emotionally honest. Do not answer "excellent" to the question "how are you?", Even asked out of banal politeness, if everything is bad with you. Moreover, it's not worth it if in the morning everything did not work out for you and you look like a living illustration of the concept of "gloom". Share with others both troubles and joys.

CHAPTER 1: Disciplined Leadership

What is Leadership?

"A leader is one who knows the way, goes the way, and shows the way" John C Maxwell

Great leaders are those with vision and an ability to pull people towards that vision. They make that difference between failure and success. There have been popular debates about whether leaders are born or made. However, one thing is certain- Anybody can be a leader but leadership isn't for everybody. This simply means that one who isn't a leader but aspires to become one can learn to do so.

Characteristics of a Good Leader

1.**Excellent Communicator**- The book by Dale Carnegie, `How to win friends and influence people', stresses on the importance of this point. It explains how great leaders attains the ability to not only speak effectively in private and in public, but most importantly, how to listen and understand other people speak.

2.**Confidence**- He or She must first believe in themselves before compelling others to believe. Leaders are known to have a strong sense of power by simply being comfortable in their skin.

3.**Time Management**- Time is valuable, and leaders are known to place this value very high, even higher than money. Managing 24hrs a day isn't as simple but by creating a list of high priority task, sharing these tasks to appropriate time per day or per week, one will achieve greater success rate rather than not managing time at all.

4.**Innovation**- Leaders are easily spotted by their creativity and unique in how they think. They are the revolutionist. This must only be exercised in grandeur but in simple daily tasks. Problems arise every day whether domestically or professionally and it is a leader's duty to find a solution in every possible way.

5.**Delegation and empowerment**- This characteristic works together with time management. Leaders aware of their capacity and their limitations to execute task. This is why they need to maintain a good relationship with people. A popular quote says that a great king is one who knows his court. This means that a leader must not only take account of his abilities but also the ability of others. This will come in handy in a situation where tasks are reassigned to people- to the right people.

6.**Positivity and Energetic**- Everybody wants to be around people with positive energy. Emotions/Moods can be infectious. Robert Greene ascribed this law to Number ten in the 48 laws of power. It explains how people avoid the unhappy and unlucky as a natural phenomenon. Likewise, people are most attracted to happiness and luck. In leadership, there must be followers, this is unavoidable.

7.**Passion and commitment**- It is one thing to begin a course, and it is a totally different thing to see it to the very end. Leaders strive in this aspect of finishing what was started. They carry out their tasks with great zeal and focus.

8.**Honesty and Integrity**- One vital trait about great leaders is trustworthiness. When a leader successfully gains their follower's trust, the rest is history- they are able to move towards their vision without resistance. Leaders are great examples of what is known as "practicing what one preaches".

9.**Accountability**- being accountable means being responsible for decisions made. NO EXCUSE. Leaders know that every decision must be made wisely because at the end of the day, they must answer to a troublesome question- "What did you achieve today?"

10. **Empathy**- leaders must live by example. They must show compassion in both mind and body. Amongst all the points, this play a most important condition in being a great leader. This is where emotional intelligence come into play. Knowing and understanding one's emotions while learning, understanding, and controlling the emotions of others- hence managing the emotional affair of a course.

Leadership involves mastering oneself and the affairs of followers. When becoming a leader, it is as important to also take into consideration the different types of dealing with situations. This flexibility is applicable where a successful tactic in one experience may turn unsuccessful in another experience. For example; An employee's manner in dealing with his employer must be completely different in dealing with his colleagues.

7 Disciplines of Leadership

1.**Autocratic Leadership**- This is what is practiced by the authoritarian. Generally, all the responsibility in asserting power and authority is given to one person. There is little or no input by the team/subordinates of which the roles/tasks of each member is dictated by one head. The main difference of this type of leadership from dictatorship is that autocracy, permits only one person with complete power while dictatorship can be one person or a group of people. Example, kings and queens employs this tactic in leading their kingdoms.

This is a rigid leadership practice therefore, being clear and assertive is important for decision-making. Although it I could be beneficial in the affairs of a company or a nation, in most cases, subordinates feel powerless and demoralized. Successful authoritarians recognize and effectively address this clause.

2.**Charismatic Leadership**- This the strives on a leader's ability to inspire and transform the thoughts and attitude of others- in case of organization, its followers. The vision of the leader is vaguely adopted by the infected and all work together in achieving a common goal- that which was inspired by one person. It is Passive-aggressive in nature. For example, a church leader is charismatic in dealing with the congregation. He/she knows that the followers are not obligated to remain under the supervision of the head and gaining followership relies majorly on belief and energy. Unlike authoritarian leadership that is forceful and aggressive by nature.

3.**Transformational Leadership**-just like charismatic leadership holds its influence by inspiration and motivation, transformational leaders also adapt the same tactics of dealing but unlike the former, this type of leadership doesn't require physical presence to effect change. It's often the case when the both kind of leadership is used simultaneously. An example of transformational leadership can be found in stars and heroes. It's stories of them ignites change.

4.**Laissez-faire Leadership**- It is most common in the professional sectors where there is a high level of autocracy coupled with a degree of transactional leadership. Here, employees are entrusted to carry out tasks that are for the benefit of the organization without direct order form the authoritarian (the boss). This type of leadership is successful when a company/organization assigns the right people to a specific position. It's an indirect method of infusing autocracy. For example, bank marketers are given a target to generate X number of funds by the end of each month. However, they venture to achieving that goal is left for the marketer to decide but although, the target was originally placed by the boss and will only be altered by the boss.

5.**Transactional Leadership**- in a transactional type, a follower's loyalty relies heavily on the value of transaction. In the case of profitable organization, an employee is obligated to obey the leader when he/she accepted the job. However, when the employee resigns or the employer relieves duty, the employee will in turn be released from all obligations. Here, roles are clear and defined. Rewards and punishments are dependent on the degree of how well the job is carried out.

Note that this type of leadership is tightly limited to professionalism but not necessarily limited to companies and organizations. It could be vaguely applied in domestic circumstances like babysitting or lawn-mowing and in other cases.

6.**Supportive Leadership**- leaders using this method delegate tasks and also provide means to achieving the goal. It is a more compassionate method than the transactional type. For example, a parent/guardian pays student tuition with an expectation that the student pass that academic session with good grades. They will further into providing food and housing allowance because it may increase the chances of achieving the common goal. However, "to what degree?" is vaguely understood between the two parties. Some parents will support with only tuition and some will support to the very point of buying course handouts. Here there is also a vague expectation. If there were concrete and clear expectations, it becomes transactional and therefore loses all meaning of compassion. Professionally, it is not advisable to rely solely on this leadership strategy. Another example of how leaders employ this tactic is seen in non-profitable organizations like relief aids and even churches.

7.**Democratic Leadership**- in this strategy, everybody is both leaders and followers.

The emphasis is on equality. Ideas are being shared and discussed with unbiased opinion approach when executing plans. Members of this type of leadership are entrusted to act in benefit of all others but not obligated to do so. It encourages and promotes creativity in family, companies and organizations. An example of democratic leadership is seen in the united states of America where the government acts on fair and equal rights of the citizens.

The above listed are in constant use of a complexity of emotions. One must have mastered the emotions of both themselves and of others to be able to successfully execute these power tactics.

It must also be noted that the level of passivity and aggression in employing these tactics are flexible as well. For example, for obvious reasons, Charismatic leadership is easily applicable in leading a church, there will be cases where church workers (staff member or volunteers) will respond effectively to a transactional form of leadership. The secret is knowing when and how to apply these types of leadership.

However, what happens when emotions get in the way of successful executing these strategies? When charisma is needed to address the congregation, what then happens if the pastor isn't just having a good day?

Chapter 2: Self-awareness

When asked about the meaning of self-awareness, some would confuse it for self-consciousness. The differences between them are quite clear, and the knowledge of their distinctness would be invaluable to you. Being self-aware means that you have taken a critical look at yourself, and you know who you are. This may seem like one of the ramblings of some self-proclaimed motivational speaker. After all, how could an individual not know themselves? But self-awareness is much broader than the knowledge of your birthday, your name, or which camera angle highlights you the best. Instead, that is what self-consciousness is about. It directs the attention to the worst parts of one's self and causes such a person to hide their faults from even themselves. They would usually be afraid to walk confidently in public or speak about the things they honestly believe in order to avoid being shamed. There is also self-assuredness which is often a good thing but could lead to delusions of grandeur in extreme cases. A self-assured person is one who is confident of their abilities and may feel like they need no one else on their journey to success. They might exaggerate their potential in their minds and sever bridges as a result of pride. This is the point where self-assuredness becomes unhealthy.

Now, self-awareness is you looking at the various aspects of your life without bias. Instead of making excuses for yourself, you agree with yourself that, for example, a certain attitude of yours may be ruining your life and you need to cut it off. With self-awareness, you remove the blinders from your eyes, praise your useful traits and abilities, and work towards ridding your life from as many vices and bad behaviors as you possibly can. People who are self-aware would rarely be shocked when someone tells them something about themselves. They already know what they are doing right and wrong and hate working towards self-improvement.

One challenge on the path to self-awareness is distraction. We are living in, arguably, the most fast-paced age in the history of human civilization. We are either carried away by the ups and downs of the internet or trying to get ahead in a world that moves too quickly for many to keep up. Most people are just too consumed with getting the better of their competition (or perceived competition) and putting their best foot forward in every situation, that they forget to look at themselves in the mirror and ask some honest questions.

Below are some of the questions which could help you to know yourself much better.

In which situations do you feel ashamed, weak, or angered? What are the things you hear or see that weigh down on you? By answering these questions, you can proceed to decide which course of action to take in order to avoid or manage those bad feelings. You may have to stop moving with friends who seem to enjoy talking you down and making jokes at your expense. You may also choose to talk it out with them. It could also be that your reaction to things is what makes certain situations tense, and you may want to work on being more patient, open-minded, and empathetic.

What are some of your greatest strengths? What are the things that you most admire about yourself? Are you an introvert and cannot imagine a day without books? Is your sense of humor easily the liveliest thing in any gathering? Also, ask yourself about the skills you have acquired or the natural abilities you possess. Since the people around us could also be our strengths, ask yourself who you believe are your truest friends and why you think so. These questions are not for you to gloat, but to give you a deeper appreciation for the blessings in your life. It is a good thing to walk confidently, but it is even better to feel that way.

What would you say are your biggest weaknesses? Are there some qualities about yourself that you are ashamed of? You should answer these questions with honesty because how well or badly you perform in life depends on the kinds of thoughts you entertain. You will, subconsciously at times, act out your most prevalent thoughts, and it is for this reason that you ought to be candid with yourself. This is not to say that you should beat yourself up and be hard on yourself. Even though we are supposed to work towards it, no one can lay claim to perfection. And that's not such a bad thing. It's cool and exciting to know that there are more things for you to discover about your potential and that the best of you will always be ahead.

What time in your life brings back the fondest memories? These memories make you smile, and there's very little (if anything at all) you would change about them if you had the power to. You enjoy looking back at these times in your life, just to feel a little of that freedom, love, accomplishment, and happiness once again. Now, ask why these memories make you feel this way. Was your happiness at the expense of someone else, or did everyone have a good time? Is the memory a fond one because of a person or the people who were present? Was it because of the activities or the kind of conversations you were engaged in? The answers to these questions will reveal to you in which situations you thrive best.

Which period in your life does the opposite of the above point? Is there a time you can think back to that only makes you cringe or feel sad? Are you embarrassed by the things you did or didn't say, and wish you could have a do-over? For example, it could be an opportunity you missed, a person you severed ties with, or someone you did not stand up for. Think about them and consider what the reasons might be that such memories have taken on such a dark hue. Do not jump at the most obvious explanations but think deeper for the more foundational causes. If these memories have a tendency to trigger your Post Traumatic Stress Disorder, wait until you are in a room with your psychiatrist.

What are you most passionate about achieving? The actions people make are, quite often, determined by their dreams and expectations. They inadvertently behave in such ways as to increase their chances of succeeding in any venture. At the least, this is how people are advised and expected to act in order to fulfill their visions. So, asking yourself this question would reveal your innate motive for several of your actions. You would also know what you should deliberately incorporate into your routine and how you should respond to things in order to achieve those dreams and goals for your life. Be logical with your answers, but not afraid. Don't mention goals you believe are small enough to be easily achievable. Now that you know your strengths and weaknesses, go all out and imagine greatness.

What is your definition of success? For some, the answer is having lots of money. Others would say getting to fulfill a dream, such as publishing a book or getting a degree, and adding value to the lives of people is what it means to be successful.

Still, there are those who would object to those definitions and say that the true measure of success can be found in those you love and that love you in return. Your answer could be something different from any of those; it all depends on how you view success. What are those things you admire about the people you see as successful? Many of the decisions we take and the paths we tread are determined by our perspectives on success.

In three words, how would you describe yourself? This question is not limited to your physical appearance alone. How would you describe your personality? In the same three words, what would be your description of the past experiences of your life? How would you describe your love life or your childhood? If you know yourself well enough, you would not require unnecessarily complex or ambiguous words to describe the things mentioned in this point. When you are not looking at the mirror or the selfie camera of your phone, when your eyes are closed, how do you picture yourself? Can you see what your anger, happiness, and drive look like?

What are your core values? You hear people talk about this almost all the time, but it is usually without any self-awareness. They simply mouth what they think are the right things to say without any self-discovery to determine their own truth. The fact is, whether or not you consider yourself to be a principled or disciplined individual, there are some things we hold dear to ourselves and that steer our actions. There are limits to the things we may be willing to do and reasons why we reject certain opinions or beliefs. These values don't have to stay hidden away in your subconscious thoughts while they control important aspects of your life. Uncover and identify them for what they are. If you would have to change them is something else to be decided by you.

When a change happens in your life, how do you handle it? It is not unusual for people to want to hold on to certain parts of their lives, even when it affects them negatively or just doesn't work. It could be something as simple as rearranging the position of furniture in your house and throwing some of them out to allow for more space. It could also be a more serious situation like letting go of a partner in a romantic relationship. We get so used to the people and things in our lives that we cannot imagine being without them, however toxic they might have been. But, like it or not, nothing in life stays the same. Since you cannot run from change, you have to learn to deal with it. How does change makes you feel, and what is your reaction to it?

Hopefully, you did not read those questions hurriedly. If you did, I would advise that you go over them once again and answer honestly. Introspection is a key part of self-awareness, and, thankfully, we all are capable of it. The only rule is that you do not ask 'why' questions. Do not beat yourself up over your mistakes and work towards correcting them instead. Ask the 'what' questions. Instead of asking why your life never seems to get better, ask the questions listed above. What are the things you can start doing now that would impact your future self positively? At the foundation of emotional intelligence is self-awareness. Once you know yourself so well that you can control and predict your actions, every other challenge in life will be easy to conquer.

Chapter 3: Developing and Handling Emotions

Emotional intelligence is the ability to keep a check on our emotions and use them to improve our lives. Knowing how we feel is extremely advantageous as it allows us to manage our stress and emotions when necessary. It allows us to communicate well with people without ruining our impression or their moods.

We are all familiar with what intelligence quotient (IQ) is, but have you ever heard of emotional quotient? Emotional quotient (EQ) is simply a measure of how high or low your emotional intelligence is. Considering the fact that our IQs remain the same throughout our lives, it is truly a remarkable thing that our EQ can be developed with time and practice. But how is this possible?

Developing Your Emotional Quotient

Here are some of the ways of improving your EQ:

Observe. We must learn to observe how our emotions and behaviors are connected. The more we understand our behavior and feelings towards certain situations, the higher our EQ becomes. Consequently, this will help us understand our reactions and will help us control them in the future. We must figure out some of the unintentional reactions that are triggered by some of the emotions we experience. For example, when you feel angry, you either raise your voice and, more often than not, your fist. When embarrassed, you withdraw from your social group. You must understand your emotions and our bodily responses and then do everything you can to conquer them both.

Don't judge yourself. Judging yourself will alter your train of thought and emotions. It will make you stop expressing your feelings to yourself. You will end up lying to yourself about your emotions. To feel and to exhibit emotions is natural, it isn't a sin. Nonetheless, you must control your bodily response based on your emotions. If you keep our emotions hidden in the simplest situations, and later when you face an uncontrollable situation, you will surprise yourself with a reaction no one is ready for. Without the information about how your body reacts, you wouldn't know how to react! Thus, by feeling and understanding your emotions, you develop emotional intelligence.

Connect the dots in your emotional history. Understand how you have been reacting to specific situations in the past. By looking back at the connection between your emotions and actions, you will be able to learn how to control your emotions and behaviors where ever necessary and make better decisions. It's like creating a template from your emotional history and studying it to know where all the weak spots are. In order to do this more effectively, write down your reactions towards certain emotions so that you can clearly figure out your emotional patterns.

Practice your behavior. This may sound weird but it is a very effective technique. When you find some time alone, allow both positive and negative emotions to surface one at a time. Try to battle the negative emotions without reacting violently to them. Absorb all the positive emotions and allow them to take control of you. This way, you will learn how to allow both the positive and negative to surface, but the negative ones will not beg for a bodily reaction. In other words, you will feel the negative emotion but refuse to respond to it.

Consider the opinion of others. Don't shut your mind by thinking that only your opinions are correct. Cut everyone some slack and listen to what they have to say. You can develop your emotional intelligence by simply learning to be more agreeable and understanding. This will provide you with an insight to other people, their feelings, and their reactions. People with narrow minds generally have a very low EQ. An open-minded personality usually finds it easier to deal with situations that suddenly arise and require explicit reactions.

Become a people person. One of the major indicators of a person with a high EQ is their ability to empathize with others. You need to understand what others are feeling and help them relate and express their emotions in front of you. Be all-ears in front of people so that you can understand clearly how and what a person is feeling. You know you are becoming emotionally intelligent when you find yourself relating to what others are feeling and then amending your behavior accordingly. This can be done by putting yourself in other people's shoes, walking a mile in them, and being truly interested in what they say and feel.

Focus on people's body language. Read between the lines to know exactly what the person you are talking to is feeling. Observe their facial expressions and body language. Practice being more observant and relating their emotions to yourself.

Be honest with yourself. Make sure that when you say something, you absolutely mean it. Being emotionally honest with yourself and others is the key to developing your EQ. This will enable people to believe and trust in you. They will find it easier to understand you and where you are coming from. Nonetheless, being emotionally honest doesn't mean that you must reveal all your negative and positive emotions in public. This may simply serve to ruin your reputation and hurt your peers.

Question yourself. Ask yourself questions like, "Why? What? Where? When? How?" Questioning yourself will enable you to ponder upon your actions and question their validity. This will help you manage your actions in the future. By the end of the day when you are just about to wrap up and go to bed, ponder upon all your actions and ask yourself, "Why did I act in such a manner?" Notice and realize all the external elements that made you react in that particular manner. Start asking yourself questions such as:

"What was I thinking?"

"What else could have been done in that situation?"

"Why was I being jealous at that moment?"

"Was I acting irrationally?"

"Was this action possible to prevent?"

Once your mind starts questioning you, you will start to differentiate between the rights and the wrongs and you will be able to make the right choice.

Learn from criticism. Yes, criticism hurts. It makes you feel vulnerable and exposed. We never prefer hearing anything negative about ourselves from anyone, no matter how close they are to us. When people criticize you, they want to expose some of your negative traits. Only when your weaknesses are highlighted are you able to understand your shortcomings and the extreme need for improvement. If we believe that we are perfect and that there is nothing "changeable" about us, we are wrong. We need to look for people we know will criticize us fairly, and we need to stay close to them because they have identified our shortcomings and will help us understand our emotions better. We can either keep our emotions aside, learn from criticism, and become emotionally intelligent; or we can allow our emotions take over us.

Take complete responsibility for your actions. If you believe that you have reacted to someone in a very irrational and harsh manner, go to them and apologize for it. The shame and regret will keep nagging at you and your mind will soon learn to avoid reactions that could elicit such feelings in the future. Soon enough, you will be able to keep your emotions and your behaviors in check. Apologizing will also make you feel better and help remove the burden of guilt from your shoulders. Simply go to the person concerned and confess that you behaved badly toward them. More often than not, people are very forgiving. They will prefer forgiving and forget over keeping grudges. Emotionally intelligent people understand how they have made others feel and the impact their words and actions have caused. Without confronting people and taking responsibility for our actions, we might continue to cause destruction in our emotional lives and the lives of others.

Learn how to handle stress. Stress is the feeling of being overwhelmed by the mental and the physical pressure life places on us. To become emotionally intelligent, you need to eliminate all forms of stress from your mind and body so that you can begin to understand your emotions clearly. When a person is drowned in stress, they usually have no control over how they behave and this can lead to many negative consequences. This just leads to added stress. By constantly stressing out, we allow stress to blind our common sense, and what happens is that our extreme emotions and behaviors take over us. The two ways to deal with stress are either to go to a therapist and seek help or write down all your stress triggers and understand how to deal with them effectively.

Handling Emotions

Now that we have understood how to develop your EQ, the next step would be to figure out how to handle your emotions and ensure that they do not create a negative impact.

The following are the steps which should be taken toward handling your emotions:

Do Not React Prematurely   Let It Out   Forgive Your Close Ones

Do not react prematurely. Reacting to your emotions on the spot is an indicator that you have allowed your emotions to take you under control. This is a huge mistake because you are likely to do something you will regret. During those few seconds when your body is preparing itself to react to a specific emotion, just take a deep breath and count to 10. If your body has still not calmed down, repeat the step. This will ensure that you do not make the worst mistake of your life. It will also provide you with a sense of satisfaction since you will know that you have handled your emotions well.

Let it out. Once you have figured out the depths and the darkness of your emotions and have successfully been able to control their effects, let them out. Let out your feelings and emotions to someone close to you by talking to them and by making them understand how you feel. You cannot keep your emotions bottled up.

They need to be poured out. Talk about your emotions, write about them and think about them often. This is the best way to manage your emotions.

Forgive your close ones. The major factor that influences your emotional growth is usually your peers. It's either because of what they have said or done in the past or continue to do in the present. Maybe it could be what you have said or done to them that triggered emotions of hatred, jealousy, guilt or sympathy. If you have something against someone, learn to forgive them and forgive yourself. These negative emotions can become bottlenecks that stifle your emotional intelligence. Just detach yourself from this kind of emotional pressure.

The major responsibility for developing your emotional intelligence and handling emotions lies on your shoulders. To improve your EQ, you need to take to heart the tips given above. They will assist you help yourself.

Chapter 4: Control the Emotional Environment

As mentioned earlier, a person's workplace is probably the most emotionally charged environment they will experience on a regular basis. While developing emotional awareness–both of yourself and those around you, is critical, it may not always be enough. This is particularly true in workplaces where the job is especially stressful. The simple truth is that emotions are influenced by external factors, just as much as words and actions are influenced by emotions. Thus, if the emotional environment of the workplace is left unchecked it can create levels of stress and anxiety that awareness alone won't be able to overcome.

Therefore, in order to have a better control over the emotional state of yourself and others while at work you need to learn to control the emotional environment itself. This can be done in several different ways, from maintaining positive dialogue with everyone to establishing systems and habits that reduce stress levels when followed. In the end, the more the effort you exert to create a positive environment, the more positive everyone will become. This can help to transform even the most challenging workplace into a place of happiness, contentment and satisfaction.

Reducing stress and fear of failure

One of the main causes of negativity in any workplace is basically stress itself. Unfortunately, any number of things can cause stress, so it is actually impossible to eliminate it from any workplace environment. However, certain steps can be taken to ensure that stress is significantly reduced, thereby improving the overall environment considerably. A good way to reduce stress is to ensure that expectations are always reasonable. While it may seem positive for a person to take on more and more tasks at any given time, the truth is that people can easily become overwhelmed in this way. Therefore, it is critical that deadlines are never unreasonable, that tasks are never too large to be handled, and that goals are always achievable.

A very common cause of stress and anxiety at work is multitasking. Again, at a first glance multitasking might seem like a sign of ambition and ability, however, studies have shown that multitasking is actually counterproductive in the end. One reason for this is that when a person is faced with several tasks at once their concentration levels decrease, largely because they have their mind going in multiple directions at the same time. Furthermore, the more the projects a person has ongoing at any given time, the more deadlines they face, the more accountability they experience and the more people they usually have to answer. Consequently, this will increase stress levels exponentially while actually reducing productivity. Therefore, avoid and prevent multitasking whenever possible.

Another significant cause of stress at the workplace is the fear of failure. If a person has a goal, task or target to accomplish there is the chance that they may succeed and there is also the chance that they may fail. When success seems more and more unlikely, stress and anxiety will increase to overwhelming levels, creating a negatively charged work environment. The best way to prevent this is to eliminate the fear of failure whenever possible. One way to do this is to have an open-door policy. Any time a person is unsure that they can achieve their objective they should feel welcome to come to you and ask for help. Even if you don't help directly you can find a solution that will put the person back on track for success. Being a source of help rather than a source of judgment will go a long way in eliminating any fear of failure and the negative emotional environment it can create.

Creating a positive environment

Reducing stress and the fear of failure in the workplace is only one side of the coin when it comes to controlling the emotional environment. The other side of the coin is to create a positive environment, one that is optimistic, relaxed and generally happy. Unfortunately, in most workplaces the focus is placed strictly on results, meaning that the emotional environment becomes increasingly toxic over time. The real tragedy is that such toxicity only serves to undermine results, not improve them. However, when you take the time to create a positive environment you can reduce and even eliminate such toxicity, thereby improving results as well as the emotional wellbeing of your employees.

Nothing creates a positive interpersonal environment more than the establishment of trust. When coworkers trust each other, they tend to enjoy their job more, thereby producing better results. Additionally, when employees trust their bosses, they tend to be more productive and loyal, usually staying with the company far longer than employees who don't trust the people they work for. The best way to establish trust is to avoid any actions that diminish trust. For example, never, EVER, engage in gossip or rumor spreading. Any time you are willing to talk about other people you will be seen as being untrustworthy, especially if you appear friendly to the people you gossip about. However, by never speaking about other people, except in a good way, you will induce trust and confidence in those around you.

Another way to establish trust is to make sure you are reliable. If you make a promise, always keep that promise no matter how much effort it takes or how much you might come to regret it. When you fail to keep the promises you make, your word will become meaningless, thereby reducing the trust others place in you. However, when you follow through on each and every promise your word will become rock solid in the minds of those you work with. Such trust will create a bond that money cannot buy. The important thing is to make sure that you encourage the same trustworthy actions in those around you, thereby creating a healthy and strong emotional environment for everyone.

Chapter 5: How to control anger

Anger is one of the basic emotions, which tells us that something is hampering our path towards an important goal. Faced with an experience of anger we can react in many different ways: some people are more likely to internalize, to keep everything inside, others try not to think about it avoiding the object of anger, others to vent it with words or behavior, others continue to think about what caused the anger, while keeping the emotion active.

Once the anger is activated and we see red, we can avoid the people who made us angry, we can try to discuss the thing calmly or we can express anger towards the person or the situation that caused it impulsively and liberating. We let off steam. Someone cuts our way and we sound the horn, our colleague makes a mess and we scream against him, our partner says something too much and gets the outburst.

If on the one hand has been repeatedly shown how to ruminate in an angry way and keep the snout both counterproductive and in the relationship that for emotional regulation, we are sure that venting anger is helpful? Professor Brad Bushman says about it

"It is not given that something is positive just because it makes you feel good."

Basically, we pay attention to the usefulness of the outburst only because immediately we feel better. Bushman conducted a series of studies on the subject with his research team, arriving at interesting conclusions. One of these researches involved 600 students (half males and half females) divided into 3 groups: all students were asked to produce a written text, which was then analyzed and criticized by a partner; a first group then received an indication to hit a pungiball imagining that it represented the critical partner, a second group had to hit the pungiball thinking how much this improved their physical fitness and a third group did not receive any indication and did not hit the pungiball , waiting.

All subjects then compiled questionnaires that evaluated anger and aggression. According to the theory of catharsis, let off steam by striking at an object and at the same time thinking about a situation or a person who has caused anger should help us to lower the level of emotional activation and calm down. In fact, the opposite trend emerged: the group of participants who had hit the pungiball thinking back to the person who had criticized them showed the highest levels of anger and hostility at the end of the experiment, followed by the champion who had hit the pungiball thinking about other. Surprisingly, the control group who had been waiting without doing anything showed the lower levels of anger and hostility at the end of the experiment.

In other words, doing nothing has been shown to be more useful than physically venting to decrease levels of anger. If these results contradict the idea of catharsis, they are very much aligned with the Metacognitive Theory (Wells, 2012): if we consider the condition of "vent" more closely, this in essence provides to engage in a form of rumination angry, simultaneously striking the pungiball. Consistent with the studies of Wells and colleagues, the forms of persevering thought contribute to keeping the attention focused on the situation that triggered the negative emotion, while maintaining the emotion itself (in this case, the anger). The fact of staying still without doing anything (a condition of control for this study) has much to do with what Wells calls "leaving thoughts alone": that is, allowing thought (in this case angry) to simply go away how it has arrived, without feeding it with further cognitive and attentive resources, which keep it activated and vivid.

It is interesting to note that a study that includes so many subjects, starting from a completely different theoretical background and proposing to better investigate the role of catharsis in resolving rabies dynamics, nevertheless reaches the same conclusions of many studies on the negative consequences of thought persevering in attentive and emotional terms. This makes us think that to some extent, especially for the things that stress us in everyday life, the solution can really be learning to leave oneself alone.

Find out how to learn to control negative emotions and not let them condition your relationship with others

Anger is one of the most destructive emotions, both for the one who is the proof and for the one who receives it.

People express their anger when they do not get what they want and when they receive something they do not want. The first step is therefore to investigate this frustrating desire that has triggered anger and directed it towards someone.

Rabies also involves chemical reactions in the brain. When you get angry, the amygdala, the center of emotional processing, sends a distress signal to the hypothalamus that sends epinephrine to the entire nervous system up to the adrenal glands that begin to release adrenaline.

This substance in turn prepares the body to fight or escape, increasing the heart rate and sharpening our senses.

It's all normal if you actually have to run away or respond to aggression, but if this happens for small offenses or jokes, then you may have a problem managing anger.

Here are 10 simple tips to learn how to do.

1. Clarify before acting

First of all I would like to reassure you by telling you that getting angry is completely normal and legitimate, the important thing is that you are present to yourself when you do it.

In fact, anger often masks other emotions, such as sadness, pain, depression or fear.

So look carefully inside before deciding to act on an emotion like anger, especially if it is aimed at someone.

2. Vent yourself a little every day

One day a psychologist compared the anger to "poop". I was stunned for a moment but then talking to her I understood the metaphor.

Anger is something that socially falls into the sphere of rudeness and manifesting it in public is not nice.

But it is necessary to get rid of it almost daily, so my advice is to find a secluded place and vent your anger 5 min a day.

You can scream, beat up cushions, jump and scream, but do it in private for the "poo".

3. Free yourself from addictions

Anger is sometimes triggered by a lack of calm and serenity, so if you have addictions, from alcohol, drugs or just tobacco, know that you are fueling your anger at the expense of your calm.

Look for a professional who can help you free you from addiction and so out of anger.

4. Do physical activity

Endorphins from exercise can help to calm down. The benefits of a regular sport activity are the basis of emotional management that involves more emotions and not just anger.

There is no sport better than another; look for something that you enjoy and you like it and you're done.

5. Sleep well

Most adults need at least 7-8 hours of sleep per night. Depriving this possibility contributes to a wide range of health problems, in addition to the inability to manage one's emotions properly.

Sleeping properly will improve your mood and reduce your anger.

6. Count up to 10

We have heard this phrase a thousand times, before talking counts up to 10, but have you ever tried to do it seriously, especially when you feel the rage boil?

I give you a little help: take 10 full breaths, inhale and exhale all through the nostrils and fill the lungs well.

Give yourself time to cool your hot spirits and just relax.

7. Dramatize

This is the keyword when tension reigns. Whether it comes from you or your interlocutor, a smile will certainly not be harmful.

Of course you will not have to use brisk irony to the person in front of you, but maybe smile at your words or actions.

8. Take responsibility

Pointing your finger does not help, so even if someone has made you angry try to start the sentence with IO and not TU, even saying "I'm angry, disappointed, offended".

By taking this step towards your center, your interlocutor will first understand your emotion and, if he really acted to offend you, he will probably ask for an excuse first.

9. Let it flow

Always remember that it is your right to decide to get angry, but it is also your right to decide to continue to be all day or less.

Anger primarily hurts yourself and then others, so get angry without harming anyone including yourself and then let go of this emotion that otherwise will stop on the liver.

10. Ask for help

If after all these tests you continue to have problems with rabies, it is probably time to ask for help from a professional who can follow you personally.

Admit it, you too will have lost control and give free rein to anger. After all, anger is nothing but a human emotion, often triggered by a somewhat negative experience, from which we have come out injured or offended, or by the frustration of not achieving the goals we have set ourselves. Anger is therefore normal, but you should never lose control. Anger out of control can indeed be destructive, undermine personal and work relationships, and even compromise our health and our quality of life. This is why it is important to be in control of one's emotions, including anger, to avoid becoming chronically angry and, even at work, to destroy the relationships that we have built with difficulty. But how to manage anger? How can we endure that non-obnoxious or unpleasant colleague, how can we avoid being heated due to mistakes made and results not obtained? Here are 5 good tips.

1. Know yourself

We have said it and repeated it, everything starts from our knowledge of ourselves. Are we inclined to rally for the mistakes made? First of all, let's learn to take an example from what we have done wrong, try not to criticize ourselves more than necessary and not to complain: complaints, outbursts, criticisms are fertile ground for anger. We can never change others, those that make us angry, but we can change ourselves. Let's ask ourselves what's bothering us more, and then if that thing has always bothered us or started doing it recently. Let's try to understand if the anger that mounts within us has deep roots, or is given by a general intolerance that is telling us that the time has come to change something - work? -, to question ourselves.

2. The power of the no

Our mental health, our control of ourselves, can depend on a no saying without hesitation. If you are used to always saying yes, maybe because you are in a subordinate position, it is time to realize that saying no is possible, it is your right, and doing it will make you feel better.

3. The break

Every hour try to take 5 minutes to reorganize the mind, put your thoughts back in line. In these moments off it can be useful to arrange the desk: tidying up the space that surrounds us often helps to make order even in our heads. If you work in a very stressful and stressed environment, it can help you take minutes for yourself, out of the chaos and work routine. Then invest your personal time for sports or outdoor activities that allow you to recover physical and mental energy.

The break can also be decisive to avoid direct confrontations: if you are in front of those who made you angry, rather than replicate and risk complicating even more the situation, it is better to take deep breaths, maybe get away and return to the question only when calm has been found. Likewise never respond to emails in moments of anger.

4. Excuse and thank you

Often to avoid conflicts that could trigger anger in us or make someone nervous, whose nervousness is bound to fall on us, just learn to say thanks to those who helped us and there was close, and excuse those who he is found involved in our mistake or who we have wronged. It's not easy, but you can learn how to do it. Preventing a fire and always better than preparing to turn it off.

5. The why

A good way to quickly overcome anger and ask why we are angry, what was the trigger for our anger. If the question is serious we will need all our self-control and all our clarity to solve it, we can not afford to be angry; if the question is not, however, we must ask ourselves if it is really worth losing the stirrups for something so small.

Chapter 6: Avoiding Misunderstandings

One hundred percent of the time there's a misunderstanding is that there was not clear communication. That is a fact. There is no way that there can be a misunderstanding of both people are fully communicating, dedicating one hundred percent of their thoughts and their focus on the person they were talking to. This isn't a magical or secret in life. If you're not focusing on what someone is saying to them, you're not going to absorb what they're saying by audible osmosis. That's not a thing.

What is a thing is listening.

Feel like you're reading a book about reinventing the wheel? That listening is easy and that only a moron couldn't do this? Well an average statistic that is thrown around by psychologists is that on average, 75% of the time we're supposed to be listening, we're actually distracted or preoccupied which leads to the big lie that you'forgot' what that person told you. Did you know that the majority of people listen in order to respond to what is being said to them, not to actually understand the information they're receiving? That's not listening. Did you know that on a list of major and prominent problems polled from husbands and wives across America, regardless of gender, sexual preference or age, that better communication is always in the top five things that people would like in their relationship? We're talking overwhelming majorities here. But wait;

let's drive this home professionally as well. Did you know that during interviews, most major corporations study applicants for listening skills to determine whether they have truly developed communication skills rather than knowing how to respond to an interview or work an interview?

Let's talk about forgetting now, for a moment. And let me throw some sarcastic quotation marks around it."Forgetting." Catch my drift? The truth is that the majority of the things you"forget" that your wife/husband told you, or that appointment to hang out that you blew off, or one of the countless things that slipped through the cracks, probably ended up there because you weren't actually listening to that person when they were talking to you. You weren't focusing on them. You didn't misunderstand them and you didn't forget them. You just didn't invest a priority in them. That might sound cold, but you gave a text, someone attractive walking by, thoughts about something else, or any numerous distractions priority over what was being communicated to you. Seriously, think about it. Sure, there are times you genuinely forget, because it gets steam rolled by other things, but most of the time it's actually you"forgot."

So reinventing the wheel might be exactly what we need right now.

The key to avoiding misunderstanding is to hack off the mis and actually understand someone. Understanding is not hearing what they're saying and processing that into how to fix it, how to respond to it, or how to multitask while in a conversation. Understanding someone is focusing on them and giving them one hundred percent of your thought and mental power. By actually focusing on them, your mind is going to be processing things like, reasons behind it, how to apply this to your life/morals/schedule/etc., their intentions, and how this is actually affecting them. By focusing on a person and truly hearing what they're telling you, you will pick up far more information than you would by simply trying to form your response and thinking of when they're talking as dead time to postulate. No, understanding requires focus and mental dedication to what is being communicated to you.

Try this on your next conversation. Actually listen to the person you're speaking to. Invest your focus on them and actually listen to what they're saying, how they're saying, discern why they're saying it, and why this is important to them. No one communicates worthless facts and statements, even when it seems random it's not. You can learn so much about people by what they say to you. So when you communicate with someone next, focus on them and understand them.

Chapter 7: What happens when we don't make time for recovery?

With most of us juggling multiple areas of life within the same 24 hours, it is difficult not to feel stressed these days. In one recent study, 87% of managers questioned said their work phone are on outside of work hours and during holidays, leaving them under to really switch off.

With work cited as being the most common contributing factor to rising stress levels, it's not surprising that a lot of us feel overwhelmed from time to time. And that is the key phrase, 'from time to time'. This is because most of us are able to fit some relaxation and rest into the day. But what happens when you are feeling ongoing stress for a period of time and recovery is not possible?

When the body is under a lot of stress for a prolonged amount of time, the

Amygdala is constantly detecting threats and takes control of your responses. It disables the rational thinking frontal lobes, going into what is more widely known as 'amygdala hijack'.

Without appropriate recovery, your mind and body will not have had time to refresh for the following day, leaving you in the same state of hijack as the day before.

Think again about the water balloon.

The amygdala is constantly triggering, pins are making holes in the balloon and the water levels are going down. Without recovery time for blood cells to help plaster up the holes and allow the water levels to rise back up, the ability to handle stress continues to deplete and begins to impact other parts of the brain.

The Hippocampus is responsible for memory, motivation and regulating emotion. It is one of the areas impacted by high levels of stress. Have you ever got more and more stressed to the point where you try to vent and then lose your temper in a way far worse than you intended? This is one of the side effects that we're talking about here.

Studies have shown that the Hippocampus actually starts to shrink in the brain of those in high stress situations. This explains why many that have been through very stressful or traumatic events experience memory loss and emotional unpredictability. Scary isn't it?

The great news is that we don't have to leave our hippocampus in the dark...we can do something about it.

Through stress management and simple practices such as mindfulness, we can actually reverse these effects. Our minds are made of a pliable substance and we can change the pathways in our brains through adopting and practicing different thought processes.

In fact, we can retrain it so effectively that we can actually change the size and shape of parts of the brain. Now that is something pretty special.

Chapter 8: Verbal Communication Skills

Strong verbal communication skills are important in all facets of life. Without these essentials, one may find it hard to get a personal point across, articulate needs and desires or even compete in the business world. There are many factors that contribute to solid communication skills.

Focused Listening

One of the best ways to ensure someone that you are truly listening is to intently listen. To some this may sound like common sense, but it is a skill that is seldom mastered. Usually when engaged in a conversation, the listener is multitasking. They are listening with one part of the brain and preparing a response with the other. It is painfully obvious when a person is not wholeheartedly interested in what someone else has to say. Not only does this make the listener look uncaring, but it may also influence the speaker to go elsewhere when he needs to speak about matters.

Whether you are in a leadership role or an individual contributor, strong listening skills are essential to your success. Hearing something other than what is being said or trying to think of what to say while the speaker is talking, can have dire consequences. Regardless of the industry you work in, focused listening is a great skill to sharpen.

Asking Questions

Asking probing questions is a component that goes hand-in-hand with focused listening. Rarely does someone truly understand everything another is saying without at least asking a couple of probing questions. The key is to not ask questions for the sake of asking questions, or ask questions that do not relate to the conversation. For example, Amy talks to Michelle about a project they are going to work on together. The goal of the project is to create a high school lesson plan for a literature teacher. Michelle has never created a lesson plan and has no idea of what is included in one. The conversation is as follows:

Amy: Hi Michelle. Today we are going to prepare a lesson plan for a high school literature teacher. This lesson is for the book, Teaching to Transgress: Education as the Practice of Freedom. It is not necessary for you to read the book. We have a summary and analysis for each chapter, which is sufficient to develop the plan. There are several sections of the lesson plan that we have to write and it has a non-negotiable deadline.

Michelle: Great, Amy. I look forward to writing the lesson plan with you; however, I have several questions:

Specifically, what are the sections that we must create?

Is there a template or certain grammatical rules that we must follow?

In what format do we complete the lesson plan?

What is the final due date?

Amy felt like she adequately described the assignment and how it should be done, Michelle was listening carefully and she had the opportunity to ask several probing questions to gain a better understanding of what was to be done.

Communicating with Flexibility and Authenticity

When speaking to another, the one rule you want to always observe is that you are being honest about what you are saying. This can be somewhat of a challenge because we are taught to speak with diplomacy; being politically correct, especially in the business-world. While this is true, it is still necessary to make sure you are not sugar-coating or dancing around an issue, as this can cloud the meaning of what is being communicated. Effective communication does not require the speaker to repeat or continuously restate what is being said.

Even though sometimes one is as honest or clear as they could possibly be, it takes a little more work to relay the message. The ability to be flexible in your speech, whether to make your meaning more clear or to 'show off' that diplomacy you have been working so hard at, is significant for verbal communication success.

Practical Illustration

Jerry had to be briefed on the new company that had become a partner. When he was approached by the sales manager, Sara, she began the briefing by going over some statistics. Jerry knew how to be an active and focused listener. He didn't try to multitask or work on something while she was speaking. When she was done, he asked questions about the material to get a deeper understanding and to demonstrate that he was listening. Now he is equipped with the knowledge needed for the job and also Sara has more faith in his competency.

Chapter 9: Social Skills Every Kid Should Know

For a child to mature emotionally and socially, he must interact with people outside the home. These interactions usually take place with relatives, neighbors, friends, schools, places of worship, and other social centers.

There are some necessary social skills that a child needs to learn in the early stage of growth to effectively communicate with people. This is necessary because it is easier for children to grasp this information at these early formative years. Moreover, they are the essential skills that any child should have at the beginning of the growing years. These skills will eventually help in building confidence and resilience in the future behavior of the child.

Introducing Oneself

For a child to socialize and feel comfortable with the people in the house or the neighborhood, he must be able to introduce himself. If a child lacks the confidence to do this critical social task, he may not be able to get along with people, because people tend to love and respect someone who shows confidence. It is, therefore imperative that a child is taught this valuable skill from his tender age. He should be taught how to respond appropriately to basic questions and to give an excellent introduction to make him comfortable among his peers in any setting.

Taking Responsibilities and Apologizing

Children at young ages should be taught to take responsibilities and apologize for their mistakes or wrongdoings. Accepting their faults gives them the power to admit the fact that at some point, they were wrong and need to make some adjustments. This act of boldness can lead to the development of a better character and a sense of achievement. It also gives room for improvement as the child will struggle not to repeat the same mistakes.

Observing Rules and Regulations

It is good to let a child realize that our world revolves around a set of rules and orders that must be followed at all times to ensure that things are running smoothly. Both at home and in the school some rules must be learned and obeyed for a cordial relationship with others. To live happily, we must keep this rule and respect the right of each other. Just as we have our right so also others, we must not in any way disturb the freedom of others through our attitude.

Complete an Open Task

Most children have a habit of doing things halfway. They usually stop in the middle because they don't deem it necessary to complete the work. Children need to know the importance of completing a task on time. Stopping things halfway can lead to the development of negligent behavior and laxity. Kids need to understand how to remain focused and stay on a given assignment. Doing this effectively will help them finish homework and other household tasks in a timely and logical manner.

Obedience and Following Instructions

Children need to be taught how to obey simple instructions, sometimes when they are not in a good mood; they will rudely turn down instructions. They need to know how to say no politely when they are not in a mood instead of denying contemptuously. They should be able to give the reasons for not being able to do the given task. Also, kids should be able to follow instructions, whether at school, at play, or wherever. Kids that learn to follow instructions succeed better.

Make a good decision

Children are faced with a variety of problems every day. Equipping your child with a sense of making a good decision will help him to preserve his identity without falling under the detrimental influences of peer groups. Good decision making is an essential virtue for kids to be resilient and self-confident. Kids who can make a judgment for themselves are less likely to be deceived and influenced negatively by others as they can stand on their own. You can help a child's decision making ability by guiding him to clarify the problem and brainstorm to develop several possible solutions to the problem that is creating the need for decision making. Usually, there are several solutions to any problem. Let him realize that if a method doesn't work, he can always try something else and keep trying until he achieves the desired result.

Self-reliance

A parent should help their kids to be self-reliant. Always rescuing makes your child dependent on you. Prepare them to stand on their own and look up to you only when necessary. This action will make them grow up to be confident and assertive adults that can stand up to any situation or challenges that they may face in the future.

Confidence and resilience are vital aspects of emotional health. It is essential to teach a child how to build their confidence. A confident individual can manage their emotions and handle obstacles effectively. As early as possible, start teaching children age-appropriate skills and chores that can help develop their independent muscles.

However, making him be self-reliant does not mean that he is left alone to manage his affairs himself. He should be made to realize that if in need, he should not hesitate to ask for help from the elders. Parents should always be around to intervene where and when necessary.

Learning to accept 'no' as the answer

It is essential to teach children that they can't have their way all the time. Some kids believe that they will get what they want in the way they want it every time. Let the child knows that all his demand can't be fulfilled all the time. Lack of proper understanding of this fact sometimes leads to disappointment and frustration. This fact should be well stated for a child so that when things don't work as expected, he will be able to adjust and realize that it is part of things we have to face in life.

Sharing

Children are notorious for not sharing. They won't let others `touch or play with their toys. Children should be taught that sharing is a kind gesture that everyone should incorporate in life. Sharing is about caring for others. Therefore, children should be encouraged to be willing to share with others. Praise him when he shares and interacts with others, for taking turns and for thinking of others no matter how small the gesture.

Cell Phone etiquette

It is essential to teach kids how to properly take care of themselves in all social situations. Most especially when it comes to cell phones usage and other forms of communication.

Nearly every kind of communication is done on the phone nowadays. It is essential to teach children how to talk and greet people while talking on the phone. Children usually speak on phones as they have been taught or from what they have picked up while watching you using the phone. It is pertinent to note that only voice is used as a measure to check one's politeness during a phone conversation. A child should be aware of this fact and learn to use a phone politely.

Proper Table Manners

Good table manners are one of the most underrated things most parents forget to teach their children. Good table manners for kids are a crucial part of every meal, whether you're eating at home, or having dinner with friends. This lesson is vital because it equips your child with essential tools for social interaction. If the manners of a child are not good enough, they may not be a good companion for family meals and other people might want to leave the table.

Kids need to know how to observe good table manner: Wait until everyone is served before eating; never stuff mouth or chew with mouth open. Put the napkin on the chair, not the table, and push his chair in when finished. No reaching for food, no interrupting. Plus they should always pick up the plate and say thank you. Also, they should be able to set the table: from left to right- fork, plate, knife, and then spoon, with the water glass above the knife.

Chapter 10: Becoming Emotionally Independent

After performing the exercises from chapter 2 that help you to get more in touch with your emotions; you have probably found that not everything is as it should be. Focusing on these emotional states has already started to give you some insight into how these emotional states affect your behavior and reactions.

You might have noticed that your behavior changes in a positive way in response to positive emotions. You might have also discovered how you cope with your negative emotions (primary and secondary) and how to recognize the mechanisms that enable them. Understanding this probably gave you the chance to adjust your reactions to these negative emotions which again gave you an added advantage in social interactions both in your personal and your professional life.

It is quite easy to imagine that such skills influence the relationships you have with your friends, coworkers, and even your boss. However, while reviewing your feelings and emotions, you may notice that some emotional situations make it more difficult for you to achieve a higher level of emotional intelligence, which would further improve your interpersonal relation and your chance of happiness and success. Even if this did not happen, there is always some room for improvement.

It is important to recognize how other people can influence the way we feel. For example, the fast driver can make us feel angry or even afraid for our life. This and similar situations are very common in our everyday life. Our emotions are, to a great extent, dependent on the emotions and behaviors of others which can make us feel unhappy and even powerless. It is time to end it. It is time to become emotionally independent.

Defining and understanding emotional dependency

Emotional dependency occurs when you allow another person to affect your feelings and emotions. Most often, this emotional dependency can be seen in romantic relationships where one partner becomes dependent on the other partner's emotions and behavior. For example, if a partner feels sad for reasons they themselves aren't able to identify, they might start searching for a way to overcome this sadness through their partner. It is usually connected with the feeling of inner emptiness which they hope the other person can fill.

The reason for this can be found in the fact that such a person doesn't know how to recognize or interpret their own internal emotional states effectively and is searching for somebody who will. Another reason for why this may happen is that this person does not know how to develop a particular emotion (for example love) and is counting on the partner to provide this emotion for him/her.

This process usually means giving up your control over you emotions and transferring it to others. While this might look like an easy way out of emotional responsibility, it can negatively impact one's self-esteem, which can further damage the ability to socially interact and develop healthy relationships.

In a broader sense, emotional dependency is the inability to move away from the influence of other people's emotion to take care of your own emotional wellbeing. Taking care of your own emotional wellbeing would mean not allowing the crazy driver to upset you with his reckless behavior (which was probably triggered by his own emotions).

However, the feeling of fear in the case of the reckless driver could quite possibly save our life. If the driver came even closer to us or we failed to get out of the way; the car might hit us. Our immediate emotional response (of feeling fear) would enable us to go into fight or flight mode and (most of us) would try to jump away from the car. In this case, the fear which was triggered by another person is actually helpful and beneficial.

In this way, emotional dependency can be a double-edged sword. It is important to stay emotionally independent by staying in command of your emotions. It is through emotional independence that you are able to realize your full potential within emotional intelligence and really be your very best in social, business or romantic relations.

However, complete emotional independence from others could prevent you from detecting other people's emotion and would make it difficult to connect with others. Luckily, there are techniques that can help you to achieve a perfect balance between emotional dependency and emotional independence so that you can choose strategically between the two.

Challenging Unhelpful Thinking

A practical approach is needed when talking about challenging unhelpful thinking while still keeping a certain level of emotional dependency that enables us to grow in emotional intelligence. The best way to do this is to change the patterns of thinking or behavior that lay behind your difficulties. By changing these thoughts and behaviors, you can change the way you feel.

By doing so, you can manage the cognitive, emotional and behavioral issues that prevent you from really connecting with yourself. This will help you become an emotionally independent individual who is not affected by the negative emotions that surround you.

Being exposed to the emotional influence of others can drag you down to a level of emotional imbalance which can influence your perception of yourself and others. This can quite quickly result in being trapped in negative thoughts. Thoughts like "I must be a bad person because I was not strong enough to resist this external influence, right?"

Wrong! This is exactly the way of thinking you must challenge. It doesn't help you with anything. In fact, it robs you of the opportunity to grow as an individual and to present yourself in the best possible way. It creates unhealthy emotions which lead to self-destructive behavior.

1)Disputing (Duration 1 – 2 weeks)

Disputing is a technique that can help you challenge this unhealthy and irrational thinking. You can increase your rationality and reduce your irrational beliefs by doing this exercise for at least ten minutes every day. You'll already start to notice some results after the first few days. However, for a more lasting effect, you might want to include it into your daily routine for at least 3-4 weeks. Start by asking yourself the following questions:

1)What self-defeating, negative thoughts do I want to get rid of?

2)What specific things is this negative thought based on?

3)What counter evidence is there that shows how this belief is false (or at least overly exaggerated)?

4)What is the worst thing that could happen to me if this belief turns out to be true?

5)What is the best thing that could happen to me if this belief turns out to be false?

These questions will help you to identify and understand unhelpful thinking. Moreover, they will help you to cope with the situations of automatic and involuntary emotional dependence. With proper exercise you should be able to detect when this kind of thinking is emerging and easily alter it to healthier and more positive thinking. After a few days, your answers to these questions may look something like this:

1)I am a bad person and no one loves me.

2)I got in a big fight with my husband.

3)I have a loving husband who demonstrates his love to me every day with some random acts of attention.

4)I still would be a bad person and no one would love me. If my belief is true, nothing would really change much.

5)I would start realizing that I am not a bad person and people actually love me. This means that I am not a bad person and people do love me.

You can use these questions for different situations and different negative thinking patterns you might detect in yourself. After a while this process will become automatic and you will be able to eliminate this kind of thinking on the spot. Imagine how much you could gain if you could avoid letting someone else's bad mood influence you to start thinking in this destructive way.

First of all, you could show the other person that you are strong and independent. Secondly, this ability to combat negative thinking will help you deal with high pressure and high stress situations; meaning you'll act more efficiently under pressure. But this is just a start. Combining the skills and knowledge that you have learned about monitoring and controlling your emotions will help you to understand people around you in all situations.

Chapter 11: Managing Yourself

Now that you are aware of your own emotions you need to begin the process of managing yourself. You will not be able to lead others if you do not possess enough self control to manage yourself. We talked a little about controlling your emotions in the last chapter, but we are going to go a bit further. You need to be able to keep disruptive habits and emotions under control. Poor managers struggle with bad habits and it can reflect poorly on their managerial style. Some managers never take the time to analyze poor habits and impulses, so they never even know the mistakes they are making. If you want to improve your emotional intelligence you are going to need to manage yourself and remove bad habits and impulses.

Controlling Anger, Frustrations, Jealousy, and   Disrespect

As a manager you are going to be faced with employees making poor decisions or mistakes on a daily basis. How you handle these situations will speak loudly about your emotional intelligence and your managerial skills. You need to be able to handle different forms of intense emotion and keep your cool. For example, a new employee makes a calculating mistake on a sales report, which gets you reprimanded by your superiors. You can handle the situation in two ways. First you can scold the employee and let your emotions become exposed. Or you can show the employee where the mistake was made, and calmly walk him through the proper process so the mistake does not happen again. Handling frustrations, jealousy, and disrespect are all emotions that you are going to be faced with on a daily basis. When you find your emotions taking over, take a break and calm down before addressing the issue. Anger will only make the situation worse and will reflect poorly on your managerial style. Being able to recognize and control your emotions is a skill that emotional intelligent managers possess.

Keeping Your Core Values Aligned

When you are a leader, you need to establish a set of core values and principles that define you as a person. These core values are values that you hold true no matter what the circumstances. These values will be how you make decisions and how you manage your employees. You need to make a list of the values that you hold above all else. To get you started: Integrity, honesty, loyalty, responsibility, etc. Once you have your list complied you should keep it in a place that you can re-read it when you are faced with difficult decisions. The quickest way to lose your spot as a manager and have your office environment collapse is with a breach of your core values. If your plans and decisions are not aligned with your core values, your employees will sense it immediately and you will have dug yourself quite a hole. So whenever you are faced with a difficult decision, make sure you take out your list of core values and make sure they are all intact and you are not violating your values. Leaders with emotional intelligence understand the principal behind core values, and no matter how bad the situation they and their employees know that these values will always be in place.

Being Able To Change Your Position

One important quality that is common among individuals who have a high level of emotional intelligence is being able to put their ego aside and make the right choice. Being able to adapt and change their plan when leaders understand it is not working shows a high degree of emotional intelligence. Many leaders who fail, suffer from rigid planning and large ego. Once they make a decision, they are going to stick with it no matter how hard it fails. If the plan does fail, which most of time it will, these managers will blame their employees for the shortcomings of the plan. This leads to hostile environment and dissent among employees. As a leader with a high level of emotional intelligence you are going to need to be flexible when creating your plans and strategies. You need to put your ego aside, and challenge yourself to do what's best for your company and employees. Understand that you cannot predict or control the future and if your plan is not executing then it needs to change. When creating a plan or new strategy for your employees, make sure to highlight different scenarios. Have a best case scenario, an okay scenario, and this plan is failing scenario. If you alert your employees to different outcomes of your plan, you accomplish two different things. First, you manage expectations which allows you to lessen the blow if the plan fails. Second, if your employees understand what failure looks like and when a plan is not working, they will be able to communicate these issues at a faster pace allowing you to make the necessary changes. Always have a backup plan and contingencies in place for all your strategies. The bottom line, is that in order to be a leader in today's work environment you need to set aside your ego and become flexible. You need to make changes and revisions when necessary.

Creating An Environment Of Self Improvement

Leaders with a high level of emotional intelligence understand the benefit of self-improvement. As a manager you always need to be challenging yourself and your employees. One of the main reason that office production decreases is due to an overall complacent environment. Your employees are not challenged so they become bored and as a result production drops off. You need to instead create a goal oriented office with a focus on self-improvement. Guess what? This all starts with you as a manager. If you can show your employees how you are improving your managing styles, and you set goals for your employees to achieve, you are taking the first step to creating this environment. If you find that your office is becoming complacent, sometimes a change of pace is needed. One example that we like to use, is a strategy that a small software company uses. They choose one Friday every month, and their employees are allowed to work on any code they want that doesn't pertain to the code they work on every other day of the month. They create competitions and really challenge their employees. This creates an atmosphere of self-improvement and will eliminate complacency in their work space. The benefits are numerous, and some of the code that their employees created was actually incorporated into some of their products. So the moral, is to create an environment of self-improvement, and if you find your office is becoming complacent, try to switch things up for a day or two.

Chapter 12: Leadership, Management, Emotional Intelligence and The Power of Conversations

Leadership: Anytime you try to influence the behaviours of a person or group. Leadership is not positional.

Management: includes all the stuff of leadership but with a more focused attention on day-to-day, week-to-week outcomes.

Operating principle #1 of both leadership and management: Keep the desired outcome in mind. If your influence is not working, shift your style until the person responds effectively.

Operating principle #2 of leadership and management: What I get is what I am teaching people how to behave.

OP #3: Emotional intelligence is the oxygen of leadership and managing people.

OP #4: Leading and managing people means we have to be good at one-to-one supervision in order to consistently get the performance we want.

Supervision is working in close with your direct reports.

Coaching people to maintain and improve their performance is part of the deal.

Setting clear expectations for a job well done, checking that people understand what they are supposed to do, plus following up to make sure the behaviours are translating into performance is what we get paid to do.

Being in charge of a group's performance means you have at least two key objectives. Carry out the mission. Invest in your people to help them develop their capabilities and a better sense of self.

Supervision is about "sweating armpits" one-on-one conversations with regular team accountability sessions to focus everyone on the end in mind.

On the front line a manager works with team members to improve her/his performance on specific tasks. Sometimes the leader spends time with a team member to create a personal development program.

Situation

I was managing a team of six people. We, I thought we were doing well. But my boss - the V.P of Business Development had a different opinion.

He pulled me aside, face-to-face, in a one-on-one, respectful "sweaty armpit" conversation.

He let me know that my performance was not good enough and what the consequences would be if things did not change. He showed me to lay out a plan for improvement. He asked me what I thought I could do to improve things.

He gave me a timeline to work with. He instructed me on how to work with my people to implement the plan.

His intervention was a clear, definite example of leadership, management and emotional intelligence in action -- all wrapped up in one conversation.

I knew what I had to do. I did it because I wanted to keep my job. I did it because I also wanted to feel better about myself professionally.

Sometimes a little fear is a good thing.

Give your people effective leadership by shifting your style to fit their context.

In one-to-one, respectful conversations, help your direct reports to understand what you and they are doing, and why.

Give people structure and timelines to hang their behaviours on so the work is done well and efficiently.

Give them supervision in the form of crucial conversations to help them become more competent. Help them to feel about themselves as people.

On a scale of 1 to 10 how well do you do this?

How well does your manager do this?

Chapter 13: Emotional Triggers

Well, we saw the types of emotions and how they play role against each other in what we do. But, what causes these emotions? Are they released independently? Certainly not! Every emotion is an output of certain arousals or stimuli which we call it as Emotional Triggers. We respond positively or negatively to certain emotional triggers every now and then. Some cool colors, pleasant smell, aesthetic appearance gives us a positive emotion called happiness. On the other hand an odd color, unpleasant smell, ugly appearance gives us negative emotions like disgust or anger.

Many times we decide something to buy and visit the store but we feel something else there is better than what we had in our mind and we change our decisions. We could have been attracted by the new product's color, advertisement message, package, whatever it might be; something has triggered our decision (emotional output) towards a particular company's brand, product, image, etc.

Why such emotional triggers are important for businesses?

There are multiple benefits that these emotions cause to a business and a few of them are

•When a customer is triggered by a positive emotion he keeps exploring for such experience with that company. In our case, it is the MARKETING CONTENT.

•Whenever the customer feels such emotion, he easily remembers your business (content or speech) that gave him the similar mental state before, which in turn increases their loyalty

•Most times it leads to make an impulse purchase

So it is very evident that it is the emotional triggers which move the customers to take a particular action, which is buying or consuming in the case of marketing.

Types of Triggers

Marketing psychologists categorize these triggers into two types based on their nature, presence and the way they direct us to do an action.

External Triggers – are the explicit information direct us what to do next. We see them in our daily online or offline journeys. E.g. Outdoor Billboards, Sign boards, Signal Lamps, Call-For-Action buttons on the websites etc.

Internal Triggers

The information for what to do next is informed through an association in the user's memory. Normally, marketers handle this by well thought-out campaigns through which they stimulate our emotions and to act as they intended. E.g. creating awareness about the importance of wearing helmets just by picturing some accidental deaths happened because of not wearing helmets.

Let's see how these triggers can be organized in such a way to consume them in our day to day marketing campaigns.

Chapter 14: Some people are Asleep - Awake – Enlightened

Asleep: A wild person - Lacks psychological and emotional insight, is selfish, self-centered, not motivated to change. The Asleep person is scraping his or her knuckles on the social-pavement of life. Bad diet, bad manners, bad breath. That person's life is in neutral.

Awake: A sensitive person - Socially aware; but does not adjust for personal success, content with the status quo, does what is required. A "Me First" and "You Second" kind of person. Does not push forward. Keeps his or her life in drive, not overdrive

Enlightened: A whole person - Psychologically tuned-in, makes adjustments for success, cooperates with others, is compassionate, helps out, does not harm anyone, and is interested in self-development. This person is flexible, adaptable, groomed, happy, sociable, and in the driver's seat.

Today, transform yourself. Transform your fears into strength, your confusion into clarity, your judgments into love. Transform your stress and anger into manageable limits. Pause. The worst decisions are made when you are angry. Turn the volume down on your opinions and judgments. Transform your thoughts into action, your ideas into reality. Come into your own. Emerge in your own time, in your own way. Have the courage to be. And, be the new you, with a new social self. Own all that is yours and nothing else. Be your own person. Change old habits and old patterns. Pay attention to what you want and need. Listen to yourself. The universal vibration of life is at work. The Karmic wheel is moving.

We blame others for our sorrows and misfortunes but we are the creators of our world.

Five Points Needed for Insight

You don't need two or three elite college degrees to survive life, but you **do** need to be:

Life Smart – Has a variety of experiences. Understand the relationship and connectedness between yourself, other people, and the universe, your life in the here and now, and your role in the matrix of existence.

Street Smart – Ability to handle unexpected events, to get along with people of different cultures and backgrounds while withholding judgment. Getting your needs met without harming others. Can defend yourself.

People Smart – Understand human nature. Ability to navigate humanity without being manipulated by devious people and maintain a sense of humor to turn the corner on adversity.

Book Smart – Well read. Life skills pay the bills. Having a skill to support yourself and be able to read, write and understand abstract concepts about the world and problem solve effectively.

☐System Smart – An understanding of the values of the work place, and morays of society, your government, large business systems, and the core values of the people who make everyday decisions within an organization and then thrive within an organization.

By three methods we may learn wisdom: First, by reflection, which is noblest; Second, by imitation, which is easiest; and Third by experience, which is the bitterest. - Confucius

Meeting Your Needs

Meet your needs your way. Meeting your needs guides your behavior and life priorities and leads to self-sufficiency. Understanding your behavior and goals involves gaining insight into your unmet or unsatisfied needs. If your basic needs and your security and safety needs are not met, immature behaviors may emerge when you are under stress.

Meeting your needs build confidence; improves your self-esteem and self-concept. We are all "C" students in life - half in darkness and half in light. Gaining clarity to our true self leads to understanding our needs. Establish your hierarchy of needs, one step, and then the next step. Follow your spiral staircase to self-enlightenment. What makes you smile innately?

Our inner emotions always find ways to be expressed. Identify and label your feelings. When feelings are not identified doubt and suspicion enter the communication process. When feelings are shared, the receiver feels trusted and positive. When you share your feelings there is an inner release of good faith. People have psychological safety needs; they want to feel safe when speaking with you. Talking builds trust. Silence breeds mistrust.

Feelings build trust. Concealed feelings create suspicion and doubt.

Shifting Choices

Your choices determine your development. We cannot choose not to choose. Indecision is a decision. Good decisions come from experience, and experience comes from life. Our choices in life are based on our own self worth and self esteem. Although we cannot always determine or change what life has in store for us, we can always choose the attitude we will assume toward it. Destiny is not a matter of chance it's a matter of choice. If you can control the process of choosing, you can take control of all aspects of your life. Growth choices mean you have to change. What's required from us is honesty with our feelings, openness to feedback from others, and a willingness to change. The HOW method.

When you want to influence the other person's thinking toward your point of view use "either or" questions. Use two either-or-choices – Do you want a hot dog or a steak? Do you want a bicycle or a Mercedes? Should we watch television or go to the movies? Do you want a used coat or a new coat? Should we eat the three-day old spaghetti or go out to dinner? Should we get divorced or save our marriage? When negotiating with your partner put the bad choice first and the desirable choice second.

Life is the sum of all your choices – Albert Camus

Chapter 15: How to understand and recognize your own emotions

At this point, you have learned about what EQ is, how it can benefit you in your life, how your body and you react to emotional stimuli. Now we move on to understanding what emotions are, how they differ from our feelings and how to recognize them overall. While it may seem that emotions and feelings are one in the same, they are not. They complement each other and are a necessary part of increasing your EQ.

The words emotion and feelings are often used interchangeably. This makes it difficult to recognize and understand that they are in fact two separate concepts. However, you will always have both together. Gaining the knowledge to differentiate the two will allow you to learn how to recognize what you are experiencing and have better control of your emotions.

Emotions vs. feelings

Throughout your life, you will experience emotions and feelings. For most people feeling emotions is just a part of the lie. Learning how to distinguish the two and understanding them better will push you towards greatly control over them. However, you may find yourself confused on whether these are 2 separate categories or not. The reality is – they are 2 very different concepts, but often get confused for one another. To better understand your emotions versus your feelings, you must know what the big difference is.

what's the big difference?

So how do we identify a feeling versus an emotion? To understand what a feeling is, you must understand that it is your reaction to an emotional stimulus in this case. When you are confronted with any type of emotion, you will react. Your reaction is what we recognize as feelings.

Feelings are the things people identify with and share with one another. However, emotions are something a bit different.

Emotions, on the other hand, are our responses in the physical, expressive, and conscious state. We discussed how your body reacts physically to emotions in chapter 3. Our expressive way of experiencing emotions is through our behaviors and communication. Lastly, our conscious state of emotions is how we view them internally. All 3 of these concepts make up our feelings in reaction to our emotions.

Emotions are often categorized into the big 6 – anger, disgust, fear, happiness, sadness and surprise. Each of these categories can be broken down into hundreds of more specific emotions. One important thing to understand when it comes to emotions and feelings is that there is no such thing as a "bad" emotion/feeling. While some emotions or feelings can be categorized as negative due to the nature of those emotions not making you feel better that does not make them bad emotions. What you feel and experience is never bad or wrong, how you react is where the problems can arise. Our reactions are one thing we can control and it is important to remember you will experience emotions/feelings whether you want to or not, you do not have to react to them in a way that is maladaptive.

What am I looking for?

So how do you recognize emotions? You begin by a better understanding of what the big 6 emotions are. Anger is the feeling of being annoyed, hostile or displeasure. Anger is often thought of as a negative or bad emotion, due to people not typically enjoying this emotion. Many people identify that they get "angry" when they are actually – embarrassed, feeling disrespected, not feeling heard, disappointed or hurt. Anger tends to be an

126

emotion that everyone can identify with on some level.

Disgust is feeling disapproval or revulsion by an unpleasant stimulus. This emotion can also be identified as loathing, sickened or an aversion to an experience or a thing. We can experience disgust in regards to an event that is especially bothersome to us. For example, people feel disgusted at abuse.

Fear is an emotion that is unpleasant and is a reaction to a stimulus that is deemed dangerous. Fear can be felt in an unknown circumstance, in the dark, in anticipation of pain or fear of a person. Often, anger can be a reaction to fear as a way to protect one's self. Fear is an emotion that people will experience at some point and one of the most difficult one to work through. Fear is the type of emotion that can result in an increase in adrenaline and push us towards the "fight or flight" response discussed in chapter 3.

Happiness is an emotion most of us are familiar with and the only one on the list that is deemed a "good" emotion most of the time. Happiness is a feeling in response to a stimulus that makes us feel pleasure. Happiness can come from people, experiences, things, places, moments, food and more. We often experience a mixture of happiness along with some apprehension for big events in our lives – wedding, births, moves, new jobs. Happiness can also be a confusing emotion as it can be jumbled with many other emotions already discussed.

When we discuss sadness, we are discussing our response to feeling unhappy or sorrow. For most of us, we recognize sadness as a feeling we deal with in regards to loss – of a loved one, job, marriage, etc. Sadness is another emotion that is often identified as a "negative" emotion. Sadness is an emotion that we often struggle with working through as it is unpleasant and can be difficult to face head on. Through sadness, we learn to recognize what we have and can appreciate.

Lastly, we discuss what surprise is. Surprise is the feeling of being caught off guard by an unexpected event, thing, or fact. Surprise can be identified as a "negative" or "positive" emotion for most people, depending on the circumstances. For some people surprise is not an enjoyable emotion – some people do not appreciate or like surprise parties for example. On the other hand, it is a very enjoyable emotion for other people who like to not know what to expect.

Signs and symptoms

Now that you have an understanding of the 6 big emotions and what they look like, you can figure out what you are looking for in your own reactions. Identify how you respond to each of these emotions and now you have your list of what to look for.

In order to create your own list of reactions, you have to take the time to sit down and think about how you react to different stimuli. You can create a physical list of what your own reactions are and with that list, you can better identify your emotional reactions. Now that you know how your body reactions to emotions are, you can now recognize your personal emotions.

Chapter 17: Emotional Intelligence and Communication

Communication is not done in a vacuum. It is done between two emotional people and such, it is important to use emotional intelligence to advance your communication skills.

You can't communicate effectively if you are unaware of what you are feeling or if you can't read the verbal and non-verbal cues of the one you are communicating with.

Emotional intelligence, as you've already seen, deals with recognizing and managing your emotions and the emotions of others. It will help you improve your communication because you will:

Be open to new ideas

There are two parts to emotional intelligence. The first part deals with your emotions and the second part deals with the emotions of others. This means that you must make room for others in order to improve your communication.

One thing you can do is open yourself up to new ideas. You don't have to agree with every new thing that comes your way but you do need to give yourself room to embrace new ideas. This is the way to grow. If you are rigid with your own ideas, you will alienate others as you show them that their ideas do not matter.

Be honest and conduct yourself with integrity

Another thing that improves communication is honesty. Nobody likes a liar. If you lie to others, they will take note of it and everything you say to them will be treated with suspicion. In fact, people may fail to listen to your words simply because you are the one who is saying them.

On the other hand, if you are honest, you'll build trust and this will make communication easier as your listeners know that you are not out to trick them.

Open yourself up

Everyone wears a mask. This mask needs to be removed if you wish to communicate with others. This means you need to open yourself up. If you are always closed off or guarded with your emotions, the people you communicate with will have no idea what to say to you, as they won't want to say something that will make you upset. They will tiptoe around you as it were. This will not be good for you.

If you want people to be open when dealing with you, you also need to be open when dealing with them. Don't hide your emotions. There is a difference between acknowledging your emotions and reacting badly to them. If you don't like something, don't keep quiet about it. If you do, you will only end up hurting yourself as others do things you don't like.

Be approachable

You can't expect to improve communication with others if you are unapproachable. Others need to know that you are available and willing to talk to them and listen to them. The only way they will know this is by you telling them and actually taking the time to listen to them.

Statements such as 'you never listen to me' should not be applied to you. You shouldn't be too busy to have a discussion with your loved ones and you shouldn't make up your mind even before you hear what others have to say.

See others' perspective

This goes hand in hand with being approachable. You have your perspective as far as various issues are concerned. That is well and good. Nevertheless, you also need to remember that other people also have their perspective.

Communication is called a two-way street for a reason. It means that you need to see the perspective of others as you interact even as you strive to show them your perspective.

Put yourself in the shoes of your partner and try to see where he is coming from. Seeing another person's perspective should not be viewed as a justification for him or her to do something you don't agree with. However, it will help you diffuse situations and make better decisions when you deal with them.

Engage in active listening

This is a major part of communication. People with low EQ often find themselves talking a lot about themselves or having one-sided conversations. Instead of listening, they start forming the next sentence even before the other person is done talking. They also fail to meet the other person's needs because they failed to get their verbal and non-verbal cues. This goes against emotional intelligence. You can greatly improve your communication by engaging in active listening, which entails:

Listening attentively – This is the first part of communication. You need to listen when someone is speaking. Pay attention to the words spoken and make sure you get the gist of the conversation or the main points. This will come up from time to time as the conversation goes on.

Repeating the message – Once you've heard what the speaker is saying, you need to repeat the message in your own words. This will show that you understand the message and it will give the speaker the chance to get rid of any misunderstandings.

Stating your opinion – This is the point where you can state your opinion. Remember, your opinion is not often needed. You can just acknowledge what has been said without adding your two cents.

Asking questions – You need to ask questions in order to fully grasp the whole story. The question 'why' should feature prominently in this step. You are trying to uncover the motivations and get behind the superficial aspects of the conversation. Don't take statements at face value even when you know the speaker and trust them. You need to learn the context and motivations of whoever is featuring in his or her conversation.

Recalling – Since you started by listening attentively, you should have no problem recalling what has been said. You can bring up the main points to tie the conversation up or, you can use the main points as a means to continue the conversation and build deeper connections.

It's good to point out that emotional intelligence deals with more than just verbal cues. It also deals with non-verbal cues. You cannot recognize the emotions of others if you neglect their non-verbal cues. You have to check the body language even as you check the tone of voice. This way, you will be in a position to get the whole message and respond accordingly.

Develop curiosity and learn about other cultures

When someone has an interest in you, you will know it by how they talk to you and how they act around you. They will take the time to know more about you and discover your wants and dislikes. They will show interest when they talk to you. They will not be little you or act like they have monopoly over the conversation.

Emotional intelligence puts emphasis on recognizing the emotions of others. You can do this by learning about other cultures. Yes, people are different but they all want to be understood and shown respect.

If you learn about other cultures, you will get rid of many of the biases you hold. You will be more open to dealing with various people and this will show in how you speak to them.

Engage in conflict management

Emotional intelligence does not get rid of misunderstandings. However, it does help you recognize them and work to overcome them. It is unwise to expect to be on the same page with others at all times. Human beings are not wired that way. They have feelings, thoughts, ideas, perceptions and goals that make them different. Communication is geared towards navigating all those avenues so that each individual comes out with something that he or she wants.

Conflict should not signal the end of a discussion. It won't help you to get angry and walk away. You need to calm down and talk about the issue so that you can understand where the other person is coming from. At the end of the day, you want to solve your issue not add to it. Self-awareness will help you recognize the emotion you are dealing with and this will prevent you from acting out in a way that will damage your communication efforts.

Engage in effective persuasion

One aspect of communication is persuasion. This means making other people see your point of view and agree to whatever you are telling them not because you are forcing them to but because you have given them enough points to think about and make their conclusion.

The first thing you should do is get your facts straight. Don't just issue a statement as fact. Instead, you need to state your bullet points as it were. This means giving 'weight' to your arguments by providing evidence that it is actually a good one. For example, if you want to go on vacation, you need to do your homework and give several reasons as to why you are selecting a particular vacation spot. When you persuade others effectively, you will get them to buy into your idea and this will make your life easier.

Embrace collaboration

Collaboration should not be a foreign concept to you. You should use it every now and then to foster good communication. It's unwise to constantly do things on your own when asking for help will lead to a better job.

When you learn to work with others, you get to know them better and this fosters friendship. You also learn to do things in various ways. Remember, your way is not always the best way. Other people can bring in new ideas that will help you do your work in a better way.

Also, it helps to note that tackling projects from different angles does not make you right or wrong. It just means you have different approaches. Don't deny yourself the chance of learning different ways to do things just because you insist your way is the right way. This is not the way to improve your emotional intelligence.

Communication is give and take. It is not a one-man show. Thus, you have to be aware of your emotions and that of the person you are dealing with. If you do this, you will greatly improve the way you communicate and this will help you get your message through and improve your relationship with others.

As you have learned, you can use emotional intelligence to own your mind, reduce stress, and improve communication.

Let us now look at some tips that can help you improve your EQ.

Chapter 18: Emotional intelligence exercises and tasks Emotional Self-Awareness Exercise

Assertiveness Exercise

Recognising Stress Exercise

Recognise the effects of stress exercise

Managing stress worksheet

Understanding feelings

Emotional Intelligence in team coordination

Emotional Intelligence and conflict management

The Mirror Work

Confidence Workout

You will find the tasks and exercises below this section.

Transformational Leadership EI Tasks and Exercises

Emotional Self-Awareness Exercise

Name_____

Emotional self-awareness is the ability to recognize one's feelings. In the spaces below complete each statement based on how you feel. Use the blanks to add your own feeling words.

Example:

I am most excited when I am out with my family.

I feel when a trusted friend betrays me.

I feel embarrassed when

I think negative thoughts about myself when

I am _____when

I feel _____when

I   think   _____about

_____when

I am _____when

I feel _____when

I   think   _____about

_____when

I am _____when

I feel _____when

I   think   _____about

_____when

I am _____when

I feel _____when

I   think   _____about

_____when

Assertiveness Exercise

Assertiveness is the ability to express your wishes and beliefs in a positive way. Too little assertiveness can make you a passive and when you are bossy, it is met with restrain by team members and you may be labelled as aggressive.

Think of a time when you could not stand on your beliefs or when you were drawing back from stating your values.

What happened?

What did you do?

How did you feel?

Now, think of a better way to handle that situation in the future. Write a better response and practice it.

Think of a time when you were too bossy.

What happened?

What did you do?

How did you feel?

Now, think of a better way to handle that situation in the future. Write a better response and practice it.

Recognizing Stress Exercise

List the ways you experience stress physically, emotionally, and behaviourally.

Physically	Emotionally	Behaviourally

2. Circle the ways stress affects you that are most troubling.

List two or three things you can do to reduce these symptoms or times when you notice these symptoms are less intense.

RECOGNISE THE EFFECTS OF STRESS

Exercise

You need EQ AND IQ to be successful as a transformational leader, no doubt. However, stress is an emotion which is commonly experienced in the workplace both by leaders and followers and can have both positive and negative effects on the way you work and your performance.

The following checklist is designed to help you to recognise how stress affects your relationships and interactions with colleagues, and to make you consider ways of overcoming the negative effect which stress can have on you. Many of the other emotions which you experience also have an effect on your EQ, stress is just one of them.

Work through the following checklist, answering 'true' or 'false' for each statement.

When stressed I………….

Statements True or False

1. Tend not to talk to other colleagues

2. Become frustrated with those who interrupt me

3. Find it difficult to set aside time to discuss the problems of other colleagues

4. Find that my body language becomes aggressive and defensive

5. Am less likely to notice a colleague who is also suffering

6. Tend to be less sympathetic than I usually would be

7. May 'snap' at a colleague who is irritating me

8. Make my emotional state of stress obvious to others through my statements and actions

9. Find it more difficult to participate in team work

10. Am more likely to reach my target

11. Often feel overwhelmed by my workload

12. Find that I work more productively

After completing the checklist, score your answers as follows:

1. True=1, False=0

2. True=1, False =0

3. True=1, False=0

4. True=1, False=0

5. True=1, False=0

6. True=1, False=0

7. True=1, False=0

8. True=1, False=0

9. True=1, False=0

10. True=0, False=1

11. True=1, False=0

12. True=0, False=1

If you score highly, you need to rethink your reaction to others when you are under stress otherwise you risk jeopardising your work relationships.

Managing stress worksheet

1. Eustress vs. Distress

There are two types of Stress.

Eustress: positive, good stress that comes from situations that are enjoyable. (e.g., winning a game)

Distress: Negative, bad stress that can be harmful to the body. (e.g., doing poorly on a test)

Review your Stress Diary. From your stress list, identify examples of eustress and distress in the space below.

Eustress

Distress

Managing Stress

Many stressors can be changed, eliminated, or minimized. Here are some examples of things you can do to reduce your level of stress:

Exercise	Exercise regularly. Practice relaxation techniques. For example, whenever you feel tense, slowly breathe in and out for several minutes.
Nutrition	Eat a balanced diet daily. Eat more whole grains, nuts, fruits and vegetables. Substitute fruits for desserts. Choose foods that are low in fat, sugar, and salt.

Sleep	In a typical week, get sufficient sleep to wake up refreshed.

Do not use medication or chemical substances (including alcohol) to help you sleep. |
| Stimulants | Avoid caffeine, nicotine, sugar, and cola.

Do not use medication or chemical substances (including alcohol) to reduce your anxiety or to calm you down. |
| Support System | Have one or more friends with whom you can share personal matters.

Talk with friends or |

	someone you can trust about your worries/problems.
Nurture-Self	Keep reinforcing positive self-statements in your mind.
	Focus on your good qualities and accomplishments
	Do something you really enjoy which is "just for me" during the course of an average week.
	Recognize and accept your limits. Remember that everyone is unique and different.
Good time management	Plan ahead and avoid procrastination.

skills	Make a weekly schedule and try to follow it.
	Set realistic goals.
	Set priorities.
Relax	Take a warm bath or shower.
	Go for a walk.
	Get a hobby or two. Relax and have fun.
	Get in touch! Hug someone, hold hands, or stroke a pet.
	Physical contact is a great way to relieve stress.

Stress Management ii

Think about how to cope with and prevent the distress you identified in your Stress

Diary and the questions above. Describe your plan for coping with distress in the space below.

Exercise	
Nutrition	
Sleep	
Stimulants	
Support System	

Nurture-Self	
Good time management skill	
Relax	
Other	

UNDERSTAND FEELINGS EXERCISE

Description

This exercise has been designed to help you reflect on real issues in your past when you were at odds with another individual. Being able to understand how others feel and why is vital to most areas of life. Managing relationships, whether personal or in the workplace, cannot be successful unless you understand individual motivations.

Task

Identify a situation where someone reacted in a way that caused you surprise, disappointment or hurt. It could be a personal situation or in the workplace.

1. Briefly outline what happened.

2. What did they say?

3. How did they say it? Describe their tone of voice?

4. Describe their body language.

5. How would you label the emotions they may have been feeling?

6. What might have been the trigger?

7. Was there anything you did or said that might have exacerbated the situation?

8. Could you have recognised their feelings earlier in the interaction? Did they give

any clues early on that they were concerned or upset?

9. What could you have done to positively influence the situation?

10. What have you learned that you could apply in the future?

ASSESS EMOTIONAL INTELLIGENCE OF YOUR TEAM

Description

Emotional intelligence is central to the way in which teams work.

Task

1. Answer the individual questions on your own

1a. Individually – Creating Awareness of Emotions

Do you always take the time to ask how other team members are getting on?

Are you open with colleagues?

Do you make an effort to engage quieter team members in conversation?

1b. Individually – Regulating Emotions

Would you confront bad behaviour?

Do you offer support to other team members and 'stick up' for weaker team members?

Do you listen to opinions which are different from your own?

Are you always careful not to hurt other team-members feelings?

Do you try to acknowledge all contributions to the team?

2a. As A Team – Creating Awareness of Emotions

Is time set aside to see how everyone in the team is getting on?

Does your team socialise out of office hours?

Are you aware of the team displaying 'group moods'?

Are all team members encouraged to give constructive feedback at any time?

Do you ask internal and external customers how they view the team?

2b. As A Team – Regulating Emotions

Do you always set aside enough time to thoroughly discuss important issues?

Does your team deal with confrontational behaviour effectively?

Do you always express emotions openly?

Do you all allow time to relax and de-stress?

Do you always stay focused on the ultimate objective?

Does your team work in a problem-solving, rather than a blame culture?

Do you work as a team to anticipate problems?

Are you prepared to make decisions on behalf of the team, if individual team members are hesitant?

2c. As a Team – Beyond The Team

Do you take time to learn what other people in the organisation are thinking?

Are you aware of potential external sources which could influence your group?

Are you familiar with the cultures and values of the organisation?

Are your team's actions in line with organisational culture?

Do you build external relationships and take advantage of networking opportunities?

Does your team provide support for other teams?

3. Now look through the above questions, and highlight with a star, the ones which your team has answered 'no' to. Discuss how you can approach these areas where there is room for improvement.

HANDLING CONFLICT

Description

This exercise has been designed to help you reflect on real issues in your past, analyse how you responded and with the benefit of hindsight, identify how your behaviour might have better influenced a more satisfactory outcome.

Task

Complete the following:

1. Briefly outline a time when you were in conflict or felt strong emotion about something and you were not happy with either the interaction itself and/or the outcome.

2. Think back to how you were feeling at the time. Note your feelings and emotions.

3. How might your feelings have influenced your behaviour?

4. How did your feelings affect your performance?

5. How could you have played down the negative emotions and enhanced the positive emotions to ensure a better outcome?

6. How could you use these learning points to guide your thinking and action in the future?

Mirror Work Exercise

This exercise is intended to boost your confidence and will also help in reaffirming your choices. This exercise is best done in the morning and it is effective when you do it for at least thirty days consecutively.

Exercise

Do this exercise early in the morning just before leaving home or later in the evening just about sunset. To do this exercise, find a mirror in your bathroom or bedroom.

For the first few seconds, just stand there and really look at yourself, deep in your eyes. You may feel very uncomfortable or awkward, if you've never done this before, just take a deep breath and take another good look at yourself. It's just a way of getting to know you better and connect more with yourself. As you look at yourself, send as much love and acceptance as you can. Really look at yourself and see what you look like to the outside world, taking notice of your eyes, nose, forehead, skin and so on.

After you've really looked at yourself for a few seconds, say out loud to yourself "I love you" and then your full name. Repeat it again. Notice that this may bring up uncomfortable feelings but just do your best to just stick with any feelings that come up, whether positive or negative. They are just feelings and you can accept them and allow them to be. After that, then say these affirmations to yourself: (you may add more)

"I am love. I vibrate love. I love."

"I am joy. I spread joy. I am joyous."

"I am motivated. I motivate others with grace and honour. I feel the positive energy."

And finally, make these sort of affirmations to end it all.

"Day by day, in every way, I am more and more successful."

This exercise should take between 10-15minutes.

Watch your confidence, awareness and acceptance of yourself grow as you do this. Also watch positive energies surrounding you, as you reaffirm these statements every day.

After 30 consecutive days of this exercise it will become a part of your subconscious mind, and you will notice how much better you feel about yourself and how much more comfortable you are in who you see.

Have the best of days!

Confidence workout

This is purely a confidence workout and will be very helpful if you think you need some guts facing some situations or particular individuals who may be intimidating you in some ways.

To do the exercise, get a mirror on the wall (not necessarily a full body length), just one that you can see your face. Make sure the mirror is steady wherever it is placed; preferably not one you will need to hold to avoid the mirror being shaky.

Stir in to your eyes without blinking for up to at least fifteen-twenty seconds. You may not get it straight the first time but practice as many times as you can until you are confident enough and able to look in your eyes without blinking for at least fifteen minutes. Once you are able to master this practice, you will be able to look anyone straight in their eyes without blinking.

This exercise is best used when you think you are being intimidated or want to stand up to your beliefs.

Note: Please do not do this to intimidate other people. Only use it when it is appropriate.

Chapter 19: Using your emotional intelligence for better overall performance

Let's get one thing clear. Too many of us have a problem separating our thoughts from our emotional states. Whenever some sort of mental image comes to mind of somebody says something, it triggers a wave of negative emotional states. If you're not careful, you'll end up saying or doing something that you will come to regret later on. You feel that you can't help it.

You just need to think of something or somebody has to say or do something, and you get triggered. This leads to all sorts of rash actions. Chances are, if you're like most other people, you don't like this or, at least, you shouldn't. This all boils down to an improper analysis of whatever it is that triggered you.

It doesn't matter whether it's a thought or a word somebody said or something that they did, you improperly analyze it and you come up with hasty conclusions and oftentimes these lead to something that you would regret. Emotional intelligence enables you to get out from this trap.

Using emotions to your advantage

The first thing that you need to do is to understand your emotional responses. This is important. You can't just gloss over this. You can't just rush through this. You can't just automatically assume that you have a problem with your emotions and this is why you're reading this book in the first place. No. You're going to have to slowly walk through what your typical emotional responses are.

You have to get a clear understanding of what you're thinking or what you're perceiving and how you respond. This is how you get out from under them. It all boils down to getting a clear perspective on the issues in your life.

Now that you have a clear understanding of how you normally react, ask yourself these questions: What kind of emotional state would lead me to a better understanding of what's going on around me? What range of emotions would help me burn less bridges? What kind of feelings would lead to more effective actions?

Remember, your analysis of your stimuli is what triggers these range of emotions. By looking at the emotions that you want to end up with, you can then walk back from that point to a better analysis. That raises the question: how should I read the things that normally trigger me, so I can end up with these more positive emotions?

Understand how you interpret your emotions

You have to take control of how you analyze the things that are happening around you. Now, this is easier said than done, especially if you tend to react habitually. Still, it can be done. How? First, you need to avoid jumping to conclusions. Don't automatically assume that there is only one way to read the situation.

For example, somebody came up to you and said you're ugly. Is there only one way to respond to that? Similarly, if somebody said you're fat or you have back acne, what then? Avoid jumping to conclusions. The conclusion here, of course, is that you should push back.

There are other ways to deal with stimuli. When you do this, you open yourself to more opportunities. I know that this is difficult because you're going to have to overcome your very natural instinct of self-preservation. Nobody likes being hurt. Nobody likes to be made to feel small, ugly or unwanted.

But you would have to overcome that to see the opportunities in front of you. If a positive reading is impossible, at least go for a neutral reading. Go for an interpretation that is not going to lead to you feeling small, insulted or degraded.

Do yourself a big favor by avoiding these

You would do yourself a very big favor by avoiding the following. First, you have to get rid of whatever victim narratives you choose to believe about yourself. I know this might come as a bit of a shock, but you are not a victim. If you're a victim, things happened to you. You can't make things happen. You are always at the receiving end of life. You know that that's not true.

The fact that you have chosen to read this book is testimony to the fact that you're not as big of a victim as you think you are. Another narrative that you need to avoid is the idea that there is always constant conflict and that is all you deserve. No.

You deserve better. Thing don't have to end up with some sort of win-lose situation.

For you to win, somebody doesn't necessarily have to lose, and vice versa. Don't think that people are out to get you or the that the best things have been taken by other people and the only way to get ahead is to take from somebody else. Believe it or not, there is such a thing as win-win. That it the opportunity that I want you to train your mind on.

Unfortunately, you need a tremendous amount of emotional intelligence to find the win-win situation in most interpersonal interactions. The good news is that it's always present. There is always a win-win. I mean it's not always going to be bright and obvious, but it's always there. It's your job to look for it.

Finally, you need to let go of an ego-centered narrative. I hate to be the one to break this to you, but the world is not about you. The world existed before you born and guess what? It's going to continue to exist long after you're dead. A little bit of selflessness enables you to see a bigger picture.

That bigger picture is not all about your emotions, how you feel small, how you were abused and how you were made to feel embarrassed. It's something bigger than that. The more you identify with something that is bigger than you, the more you grow up emotionally.

All of these narratives that you need to avoid also present perfect opportunities for you to increase your emotional intelligence. The more you work to avoid these narrative and dismantle them in your mind and heart, the more progress you make in becoming a more emotionally mature person.

Chapter 20: Develop your Listening Skills

Understand that everyone wants to be heard.

To develop emotional control and engage in fruitful interactions in any environment, you must understand that everyone has an opinion, and all people seek to express themselves in some form or another.

Being a good listener means that you give each person a chance to speak, and be receptive to hearing them out. An open minded approach is best. Avoid being in a mad rush to express your views. Avoid coming up with a response before you even hear the full message. Give others a chance to be heard.

Look at the overall message.

To be a good listener, you have to listen to the central message behind what anyone says with objectiveness to interpret better. Many conflicts exist in the world due to a lack of understanding among people. When we misunderstand others, it is easy to become angry, resentful, sad, envious, or any other number of negative emotions. These emotions can result in unnecessary stress. Sometimes, we as human beings take things personal as people that are not, and this can affect one's emotional state and response.

Some people prefer to express themselves in few words, while others many express themselves using many. No matter the length of the message, learn to concentrate on what the speaker means.

Consider Tone of Voice and Style of speech.

Did you know that Your tone of voice and the way that you speak can make you feel different emotions? If you find that your feelings are escalating at an abnormal pace during a conversation, it is nice to take a quick evaluation of how you are speaking. Bring your level of speech down to a soft, steady tone if you get feelings of anger, panic, grief, and worry under control.

If you are the type of person to find yourself cursing when you become angry or upset, learn to find different ways to express yourself. After all, swear words and negative statements are usually just word substitutes that human beings use instead of fully expressing their actual feelings at the time. At first, such words may seem to relieve the pressure by allowing the person to express something strongly. However, these "choice words" usually end up conjuring more of the bad emotions you are probably trying to steer away from. Practice working on saying exactly what's on your mind, so you do not have to yell and curse your way to understanding.

Avoid Jumping to an Emotional Response.

Why is it that so many people find themselves jumping to an emotional response when they should be simply listening? It can be tough, if not impossible, to hear what another person is saying if you are caught up in your emotions. If you speak too quickly, you can disturb the flow of thoughts of the other person, but you will break your listening pattern.

Moreover, then, you are likely to hear Less of what someone is saying rather than More.

If you want to give appropriate responses, gain accurate information, you have to halt the flow of emotions that often comes with listening. Even if you are hearing something negative about yourself or someone else, it is good to be open minded and listen objectively before forming a response. Lots of times, taking a moment to walk off or to think simply about the situation before making a negative response can save you unnecessary stress and tribulation.

Chapter 21: Being Proud to be Authentic

I remember someone once telling me that they didn't agree with my opinion on something and I thought about it for a while and worked out that as far as my life was concerned, my views were valid. I am the first person to take criticism and use it to improve myself, though fundamentally, each person has an authentic side to them – especially those who exhibit emotional intelligence. They will agree to differ, and they will appreciate that other people's opinions matter as much to them like their opinion matters to their own authenticity.

If you dress in a certain way because you want to conform to some given standards, are you happy in those clothes? If you are, then you are being authentic. Have you ever watched someone who wears fashionable clothing which isn't comfortable in those clothes? I know that people who wobble on high heeled shoes are not being authentic. They are trying to conform to standards they think are better than their own. Have you ever heard someone trying to explain something about themselves and stumbling because they are not just being themselves? They are trying to use words and phrases that will impress their listeners.

How authentic are you? You need to look at aspects of your life that matter. People who are important in your life accept you as the person that you are. People who don't particularly like you cannot be drawn into liking you merely because you put on a show. That's not authentic and the people you are trying to impress really don't care about your authentic side because they haven't seen it. Often, when you meet new people, you try to show the best side of your character. Unfortunately, what comes across sometimes is that you step into a make-believe person who doesn't make mistakes, or who fits the frame. Let me explain. If you had a portrait of the Mona Lisa and placed it into a plastic frame in red, it would look out of place. It wouldn't be authentic and would be viewed as a mistake in judgment. Now, if you placed the Mona Lisa into a traditional frame, people accept and even praise it because it's in keeping with what the Mona Lisa is. You have to frame yourself how you are, rather than how you think other people fancy to see you if you want to be your authentic self.

This is only a short chapter, but it teaches you a lot about emotional intelligence. Look at the way that you behave in the presence of others. Are you authentic? Can people trust you to be who you purport to be? When you learn to trust yourself, all the rest follows. You need to get to that point when you are comfortable with who you are if you want to up the ante when it comes to emotional intelligence. There is no show. There is no pretense. There is, however, the ability to listen, the ability to behave in the right way given the circumstances and the ability to be comfortable with your response to life. If you are not, you have some work to do to get there, but if you look at your relationships with others, these give you a lot of clues. If, for example, you don't get on with someone, find out why? Ask yourself the reasons and justify them sufficiently so that you are comfortable with your decision. You may find that being authentic is harder than you think, but it is well worth the effort. People will like you for who you are and will trust you because they know exactly where they stand with you. When you face a situation that makes you feel awkward, explore it so that you can develop your character to be able to deal with all circumstances, regardless of how uncomfortable they made you in the past. This is your chance to shine.

CHAPTER 22: THERE WILL BE TOUGH TIMES, TOO

I am a positive thinker and this book is about the benefits of adapting to such thought processes but it would be remiss of me not to point out that converting the mind to a different way of thinking will not be without its problems. It is all too easy to lay out all the benefits of positive thinking, but you live in a real world and simply changing your mindset is not going to make every problem go away.

There will be times when disaster strikes and you struggle to see anything for which you can feel grateful. To make matters worse, the old enemy negativity that you thought you had beaten, will suddenly reappear with even more addictive thoughts to temp you with. This dark place is somewhere we all find ourselves from time to time, and sometimes just knowing that helps us get through them. Being positive means that we suddenly find ourselves rich with unexpected benefits. It does not make us invulnerable.

The dark times usually come when we least expect them and it does not always need to be some major calamity that brings them on. Sometimes we can be attacked by depression and negative feelings for no obvious reason. Knowing that we are not alone in suffering these setbacks does help but it may take more than that to begin to turn the crisis around.

Firstly go back to the basics you started with in this book. You may not feel like generating positive thoughts and looking for things to be grateful for. That does not matter. Even though you don't feel it, fake it. Force yourself through all those depressing thoughts and counter them with positive statements. If you have been through some sort of disastrous set back then review it and look for ways that you could avoid having the same outcome if the situation were to reoccur. That review in itself will be a step toward the positive. Be grateful for that. Now look for something else to be grateful for. Tell yourself what a positive person you are and how you are bigger than this problem you are confronting. Be grateful for that. Slowly, painfully perhaps, the positive person you once were will begin to re-emerge, stronger and more positive than ever.

Just as learning a new instrument can be a lifelong journey keep the end goal in mind and believe in the end result. The process of changing how you think and how you view things will begin within days of deliberately following the steps laid out in this book. It may take you the rest of your life to become perfect at it. With each step forward, each negative thought or image you beat, you become a stronger more rounded human being.

"You're going to go through tough times — that's life. But I say nothing happens to you, it happens for you."

Joel Osteen.

Chapter 23: Learn How to Command & Master Your Emotions

Going through everyday life is hard, because you have to deal with everyday emotions. If you are like me, then I know that you have many emotions that you express throughout your day. I would like to take the time to tell you how you can learn to command and master your emotions. No, you do not have to go to a therapist or nothing like that; you just have to learn that emotions are, only meant, to be carried out to a certain extent.Let's begin with talking about sadness. I know that occasionally you have something in your life that causes you to feel sad, down and out.

I have learnt that at what something happens in your life you should just go with the flow. Even though you may be sad, you still have to live your life and move on. I know that, at the particular moment you feel like you could cry a river, and you should, but once you get it all out of your system, you should be able to look at the situation from another point of view. The outside view, where you take the time to look at the situation from a wider angle, sometimes you are not able to prevent things from happening, sometimes situations are destined to occur and you can't do anything about it. That is part of life that you should just face and grow on.

However, if there is something that you can do to prevent from being sad you should. Think about the things that make you sad and try to avoid them altogether, if you avoid the things that make you sad then you will not have to go through the hassle of dealing with those painful emotions. The next emotion that I would like to talk to you about is happiness or joy. Happiness is at what time you can't stop smiling for anything in the world. It's as if someone painted a smile on your face and you just can't take it off. If you experience happiness, then you are one of the lucky ones, because most people don't even smile or laugh. I guess they don't have anything to smile or laugh about.

Otherwise, something is seriously wrong in the mind. If you share the happiness you have with others make sure that you do not express your happiness too much. If you do then your friends may think that you are a little crazy. However, if you do not have any happiness, then you should work on finding things that make you feel a sense of happiness and start building on them so that you too can be happy with all the rest of us. There is one emotion that I know is in every household, and that is anger. At what time things don't go your way, you start blaming everyone else for your bad day. At this point, you shouldn't, if something makes you mad, cuss it out or beat it up, and don't blame the other people in your household because they are not the ones that made you mad.

If one of your family members is to blame then you should avoid punishing them and go for a walk or a drive just to get away from things. Most times when a person is mad it is because they fail to have control of their minds. Anyone striking out at another person is only showing that he/she is not the master of his/her emotions and something within is in command. Do you know how to master and command your emotions?

Chapter 24: The Habits of Self- Awareness

Self-awareness is a key element of emotional intelligence as it allows you to recognize mood, emotions, and feelings. Recognizing them is important since this will allow you to control them and contain the bad ones.

These are the habits that show how confident and assured emotionally intelligent people are with their own emotions.

1. They pay attention to what they feel.

Emotionally intelligent people do not ignore what they feel because they know that what lingers inside of them can grow into something too painful or too overwhelming to contain. They pay attention because they want to suppress the negative emotions while they are still containable. At the same time, they also want to enjoy every ounce of their good feelings while they last.

Application: Don't shrug off the bad feelings you have because they will inevitably come back when left unresolved. Furthermore, not enjoying every minute of the good feelings you have is wasting an opportunity to de-stress and strengthen your self-love.

2. They fully understand their feelings.

They don't self-doubt what they feel because they are attuned to their inner selves. They always try to understand if what they feel is a good or a bad thing because the action they need to take depends on it. Whenever there is confusion, they allot sufficient time to study what they feel and what they want to do about it.

Application: Emotional confusion is the first stage of mental confusion. To be truly confident about yourself and in making decisions, you have to learn what your real emotions are at specific situations.

3. They identify what gives them emotional troubles.

Everyone looks forward to achieving inner peace and happiness in life, but emotionally intelligent people exert extra effort to actually do something about it. The first step they take is that they eliminate the triggers and reasons of their emotional troubles. They recognize these things as extra baggage that don't contribute anything to their growth.

Application: As you already understand your emotions, think about the people or things that make you anxious, mad, uncertain, insecure, upset, helpless, frustrated and discontented. Avoid them as much as you can. Also, think about those that make you happy, calm, confident, proud and contented. Find them and make sure you have some around you, especially during hard times.

4. They match their emotions with the right level of energy.

They maintain a conscious effort to show the energy equivalent to their feelings. They rein their energy whenever they feel bad to avoid outburst of anger, but they also exert more energy whenever they feel good to communicate their happiness and make it a contagious disease. Matching emotions with the right amount of energy is a crucial step in preventing the conveyance of wrong message.

Application: Control the energy you put in every emotion you have. It shouldn't be too much to avoid coming across as aggressive. This can prevent you from offending other people, as well. It should not also be too less to make sure that you send the exact message that you want to convey. You don't want people to continue harassing and abusing you because you cannot convey anger or disappointment, the same way you don't want people to think that you are ungrateful because you cannot display happiness and contentment enough.

5. They hold themselves accountable for their own emotions and actions.

Blaming other people for what they feel and do is useless because at the end of the day, they are the ones who control their own emotions and actions are. They understand that so they ask themselves why they think and feel the way they do rather than ask other people why they made them think and feel that way.

Application: Control your emotions and actions to avoid hurting yourself and other people. Small things should not be magnified with overacting retaliations because broken relationships are hard to mend. Change the way you react first before trying to change the people who make you react inappropriately.

6. They acknowledge inevitable changes in the way they control their emotions.

They don't fight changes in their perspectives and coping mechanisms because they recognize the need to grow and exhibit maturity in handling their emotions. They accept proper changes that make them better human beings but reject the changes that other people devised to take advantage of them. They listen to their conscience to change.

Application: After recognizing the changes that you have to adopt, embrace them wholeheartedly regardless if they are easy or difficult because you want to become more emotionally intelligent.

7. They improve their emotional weaknesses and harness their emotional strengths.

They know the aspects of their personalities that need improvement like their temperament and patience, and the aspects that they need to harness to stand out like their compassion and happiness. As they know what makes them emotionally fragile, they pay attention and go the other way as much as possible when they encounter people and things that subject them to their weaknesses. On the other hand, they get close to those who bring out their strengths, so they can continue nourishing their emotions.

Application: Identify your emotional weaknesses and ponder why they are like that. Go to the root cause and ask why you feel that way. Think about the improvements that you can do by applying more control.

Moreover, show your emotional strengths more often because they will give you character. Show your calmness every time there is confusion and commotion around you. Show your happiness and hopefulness when the people around you are disappointed, sad and frustrated. Your emotional strengths can make you stand out in a room to influence more people for the better.

8. They appreciate all the good and bad qualities they have.

They know that they have lessons to learn one way or another. Although they are proud of their good qualities, they are not ashamed of their bad ones because emotionally intelligent people are self-assured and confident in their capabilities. They know that they can grow and just laugh about their flaws once they look back.

Application: Love your good qualities but don't hate the bad ones. Note that you can turn your worst qualities into an emotion arsenal if you change and improve them. The only time you must be ashamed of yourself is when you choose not to do something about your emotional flaws.

Conclusion

We hope the book was informative and provides you with all the tools you need to achieve your goals, no matter what they may be. The actions we perform in our lives are primarily based on our emotions and emotional intelligence. It is only logical that when people have a great sense of communication and organizational skills, they are led to have the ability to make the right decisions and interact with others. What we learn from our own emotions will enable us to persecute the lifestyle we want to live and recreate more of what we want in our lives than what we don't want. Emotional intelligence is a feature that can always be nourished and strengthened in all of us, but without having a developed sense of it, people will lack loving friendships and inner happiness, and they will generally be driven to live a life with low social value.

When we become aware of the effects and differences between EQ and IQ, we believe that EQ is often more important than general intelligence, because self-loyalty is the easiest way to live life to the fullest. In this global age, it is necessary to build a high level of emotional awareness. In the end, we all want to live a happy life and share everything with the ones we love.

However, there will still be much to learn. While it is perfectly true that some people experience serious success right out of the gate, it's also true that others need multiple tries. Expanding your horizons is the only way to find the mastery you are looking for. What this means is that you should expect to experience something of a learning curve, especially when you are first figuring out what works for you. This is perfectly normal and if you persevere you will come out the other side better because of it. Instead of getting your hopes up to an unrealistic degree, you should think of your time spent becoming more aware of your emotions as a marathon rather than a sprint which means that slow and steady will win the race every single time.

The next step is just to go out there and use all the proven strategies explained in this book. You can't suddenly become emotionally more intelligent when you read about it. Use the techniques mentioned in your daily life and see the results! You will gradually change from an emotionally challenged individual struggling with the emotions of your own and others to an emotionally developed and socially adapted individual who will enjoy better interpersonal relationships.

What can happen is you realize there's work to do. So you can make a concerted effort to improve your overall interpersonal skills by going out there and talking to people. Because without human interaction it would be impossible to achieve anything in the real world. Please do not be shy. Try your best to communicate with others simply by being honest and open. There is so much more that you can benefit from being an authentic person. Those with whom you have befriended will learn to appreciate you even more for who you are.

What could be better than that?

CPSIA information can be obtained
at www.ICGtesting.com
Printed in the USA
BVHW041045090720
583344BV00010B/806